SLAVERY IN THE AMERICAS

The Underground Railroad

Michael Burgan

Philip Schwarz, Ph.D., *General Editor*

CHELSEA HOUSE
PUBLISHERS
An imprint of Infobase Publishing

Slavery in the Americas: *The Underground Railroad*

Chelsea House
An imprint of Infobase Publishing
132 West 31st Street
New York NY 10001

Library of Congress Cataloging-in-Publication Data
Burgan, Michael.
     The Underground Railroad / Michael Burgan.
               p. cm. — (Slavery in the Americas)
     Includes bibliographical references and index.
     ISBN 0-8160-6137-8
     1. Underground railroad—Juvenile literature. 2. Fugitive slaves —United States—History—
19th century—Juvenile literature. 3. Anti-slavery movements—United States—History—19th
century—Juvenile literature. 4. Abolitionists—United States—History—19th century—Juvenile
literature. 5. Slavery—United States—History—Juvenile literature. I. Title. II. Series.
     E450.B896 2006
     973.7'115—dc22

                                                                                      200501723

Chelsea House books are available at special discounts when purchased in bulk quantities for businesses, associations, institutions, or sales promotions. Please call our Special Sales Department in New York at (212) 967-8800 or (800) 322-8755.

You can find Chelsea House on the World Wide Web at http://www.chelseahouse.com

Cover design by Smart Graphics
A Creative Media Applications Production
Interior design: Luis Leon & Fabia Wargin
Editor: Matt Levine
Copy editor: Laurie Lieb
Proofreader: Tania Bissell
Photo researcher: Jennifer Bright

Photo Credits:
Associated Press pages: Title page, 10, 14, 34; The Granger Collection pages: 5, 28, 49, 51, 57, 59, 78, 81, 90, 95, 99, 106; North Wind Picture Archives pages: 17, 18, 23, 38, 72, 93, 104, 105; New York Public Library, Astor, Lenox and Tilden Foundations pages: 27, 37, 44, 61, 66; The Bridgeman Art Library pages: 71, 83; Getty Images page: 87

Printed in the United States of America

VB PKG 10 9 8 7 6 5 4 3 2 1

This book is printed on acid-free paper.

✓ 10/4/08

PREVIOUS PAGE:

This 1898 illustration of Levi Coffin, center background, and his wife, Catherine, center foreground, assisting slave escapees in Indiana was used as a frontispiece for the book *The Underground Railroad from Slavery to Freedom,* by Wilbur Siebert.

Contents

Preface to the Series

Philip Schwarz, Ph.D., *General Editor*

In order to understand American history, it is essential to know that for nearly two centuries, Americans in the 13 colonies and then in the United States bought imported Africans and kept them and their descendants in bondage. In his second inaugural address in March 1865, President Abraham Lincoln mentioned the "250 years of unrequited toil" that slaves had endured in America. Slavery lasted so long and controlled so many people's lives that it may seem impossible to comprehend the phenomenon and to know the people involved. Yet it is extremely difficult to grasp many aspects of life in today's United States without learning about slavery's role in the lives and development of the American people.

Slavery probably existed before history began to be recorded, but the first known dates of slavery are about 1600 B.C. in Greece and as early as 2700 B.C. in Mesopotamia (present-day Iraq). Although there are institutions that resemble slavery in some modern societies, slavery in its actual sense is illegal everywhere. Yet historical slavery still affects today's free societies.

Numerous ancient and modern slave societies were based on chattel slavery—the legal ownership of human beings, not just their labor. The Bible's Old and New Testaments, as well as other ancient historical documents, describe enslaved people. Throughout history, there were slaves in African, Middle Eastern, South Asian, and East Asian societies, as well as in the Americas—and of course, there were slaves in European countries. (One origin of the word *slave* is the medieval Latin *sclavus,* which not only means "slave" but also "Slav." The Slavs were people of eastern Europe who were conquered in the 800s and often sold as slaves.)

This drawing shows slaves carrying their master in a garden in ancient Rome. Slaves were a part of many societies from ancient times until the mid-1800s.

People found as many excuses or justifications for enslaving other people as there were slaveholding societies. Members of one ethnic group claimed that cultural differences justified enslaving people of another group. People with long histories of conflict with other groups might conclude that those other people were inferior in some cultural way. Citizens of ancient Greece and Rome, among others, claimed they could hold other people in bondage because these people were "barbarians" or prisoners of war. Racism played a major part in European decisions to enslave Africans. European colonists in the Americas commonly argued that Africans and their descendants were naturally inferior to Europeans, so it was morally acceptable to enslave them.

New World slavery deeply affected both Africa and the Americas. African society changed dramatically when the Atlantic slave trade began to carry so many Africans away. Some African societies were weakened by the regular buying or kidnapping of valued community members.

Western Hemisphere societies also underwent extraordinary changes when slavery of Africans was established there. Black slavery in North America was part of society from the earliest colonial settlements until the end of the U.S. Civil War. Many people consider the sale of about 20 Africans in Jamestown, Virginia, in 1619 the beginning of African slavery in what became the United States. American Indians and, later, Africans also were enslaved in Spanish colonies such as today's Florida and California and the islands of the Caribbean.

In early to mid-17th-century colonial North America, slavery developed slowly, beginning in Maryland and Virginia and spreading to the Carolinas in the 1670s. Southern colonists originally relied on white European servants. However, many of these servants had signed contracts to work only for a certain number of years, often to pay for their passage to North America. They became free when these contracts expired. Other servants rebelled or escaped. When fewer Europeans were available as servants, the servants' prices rose. The colonists hoped to find a more easily controlled and cheaper labor supply. European slave traders captured and imported more Africans, and slave prices dropped.

Soon, American plantations became strong markets for enslaved Africans. Tobacco plantation owners in the colonies around Chesapeake Bay—Maryland, Virginia, and North Carolina—and rice growers in South Carolina pressured slave traders to supply more slaves. In time, more and more slaves were kidnapped from their homes in Africa and taken to the colonies in chains to cultivate crops on the growing number of Southern plantations. Slaves were also taken to the Northern colonies to be farm workers, household servants, and artisans. In 1790, the U.S. enslaved population was less than 700,000. By 1860, it had risen to 3,953,750.

Similar circumstances transformed the Caribbean and South American societies and economies into plantation economies. There was a high demand for sugar in Europe, so British, French, Spanish, Portuguese, and other European colonists tried to fill that need. Brazil, a Portuguese colony, also became a thriving coffee-producing region. As the sugar and coffee planters became successful, they increased the size of their plantations and therefore needed more slaves to do the work. By 1790, Brazil was the largest American colonial slave society—that is, a society whose economy and social structure were grounded in slavery. Some 1,442,800 enslaved people lived in Brazil in 1790—twice the number that lived in the United States. Brazil's slave population grew slowly, however; in 1860, it was still only about 1,715,000. However, South American slaves were forced to work extremely hard in the tropical heat. The death rate of Caribbean and South American plantation workers was much higher than that of the North American slaves. Occasionally, a North American slave owner would threaten to sell unruly slaves to the West Indies or South America. Enslaved people took the threat seriously because the West Indies' bad reputation was widespread.

It is estimated that at least 11.8 million people were captured and shipped from Africa to the Americas. Many died during the slave ship voyage across the Atlantic Ocean. About 10 million survived and were sold in the Americas from 1519 to 1867. Nearly one-third of those people went to Brazil, while only about 3.8 percent (391,000) came to North America.

If the 1619 "first Africans" were slaves—the record is not completely clear—then there was a massive increase of the enslaved North American population from 20 or so people to nearly 4 million. In 1860, known descendants of Africans, both enslaved and free, numbered approximately 4.5 million, or about 14 percent of the U.S. population.

Slaveholders thought several numbers best measured their social, political, and economic status. These were the number of human beings they owned, the money and labor value of those people, and the proportion of slaveholders' total investment in human beings. By the 1800s, Southern slaveholders usually held two-thirds of their worth in human property. The largest slave owners were normally the wealthiest people in their area. For example, one Virginian colonist, Robert "King" Carter, who died in 1733, owned 734 slaves.

Consider what it took for slavery to begin in North America and to last all the way to 1865 in the South. This historical phenomenon did not "just occur." Both slave owning and enslaved people made many decisions concerning enslavement.

Should people hold other people in lifetime bondage? Could Africans be imported without damaging American colonial societies? Should colonists give up slavery? It took many years before Americans reached consensus on these subjects. White people's consensus in the North eventually led to the outlawing of slavery there. The Southern white consensus was clearly proslavery. Enslaved peoples had to make different decisions. Should slaves resist slavery individually or in groups? Should they raise families when their children were likely to live and die in bondage? Over the two centuries in which North American slavery existed, enslaved people changed their opinions concerning these questions.

Some white colonists initially tried to own Indian slaves. However, because the Indians knew the local environment, they could escape somewhat easily, especially because their free relatives and friends would try to protect them. Also, European diseases simply killed many of these Indians. Once European enslavement of American Indians died out in the 18th century, Africans and their African-American descendants were the only slaves in America. The Africans and their children were people with a history. They represented numerous African societies from West Africa to Madagascar in the western Indian Ocean. They endured and survived, creating their own American history.

When Africans began families in North America, they created a new genealogy and new traditions regarding how to survive as slaves. They agonized over such matters as violent, or even group, resistance—if it was unlikely to succeed, why try? By the 1800s, they endured family losses to the interstate slave trade. Black families suffered new separations that often were as wrenching as those caused by the journey from Africa. Large numbers of black Americans were forced to move from the older (Upper South) states to the newer (Deep South) territories and states. They were often ripped from their families and everything they knew and forced to live and work in faraway places.

This undated illustration of pre–Civil War life depicts African men being held in slave pens in Washington, D.C., about 1850.

There was only so much that African-American people could do to resist enslavement once it became well established in America. People sometimes ask why slaves did not try to end their bondage by revolting. Some did, but they rarely succeeded in freeing themselves. Most individual "revolts"—more accurately termed resistance—were very localized and were more likely to succeed than large-scale revolts. A man or woman might refuse to do what owners wanted, take the punishment, and find another way to resist. Some were so effective in day-to-day resistance that they can be called successful. Others failed and then decided that they had to try to find ways to survive slavery and enjoy some aspects of life. Those who escaped as "fugitives," temporarily or permanently, were the most successful resisters. Frederick Douglass and Harriet Tubman are the most famous escapees. Solomon Northup was unique: He was born free, then kidnapped and sold into slavery. Northup escaped and published his story.

Although inhumane and designed to benefit slave owners, slavery was a very "human" institution. That is, slaveholders and enslaved people interacted in many different ways. The stories of individuals reveal this frequently complex human interaction.

There were, for example, in all the Southern states, free African Americans who became slave owners. They protected their own family members from slavery, but owned other human beings for profit. One such black slave owner, William Johnson of Mississippi, controlled his human property using the same techniques, both mild and harsh, as did white slave owners. Robert Lumpkin, a slave trader from Richmond, Virginia, sold thousands of human beings to

Deep South buyers. Yet Lumpkin had a formerly enslaved wife to whom he willed all his Virginia, Alabama, and Pennsylvania property in 1866. Lumpkin sent their children to Massachusetts and Pennsylvania for their education and protection. He also freed other slaves before 1865. How could men such as these justify protecting their own families, but at the same time separating so many other families?

The Thirteenth Amendment ended slavery in the United States. However, former slaves were often kept from owning property and did not share the same rights as white Americans. Racist laws and practices kept the status of black Americans low. Even though slavery ended well over a century ago, the descendants of slave owners and of slaves are still generally on markedly different economic levels from each other.

The Civil War and Reconstruction created massive upheaval in Southern slave and free black communities. In addition, slave owners were often devastated. African Americans were "free at last," but their freedom was not guaranteed. A century passed before their legal rights were effectively protected and their political participation expanded. The Reverend Martin Luther King's "I have a dream" speech placed the struggle in historical context: He said he had a dream that "the sons of former slaves and the sons of former slave owners will be able to sit down together at the table of brotherhood." (Today, he would surely mention daughters as well.) The weight of history had already delayed that dream's coming to pass and can still do so. Knowing the history of slavery and emancipation will help fulfill the dream.

Introduction

For many African-American slaves in the first half of the
19th century, the only path to freedom lay in escape
and a perilous journey north along the Underground Railroad.

A s Europeans first settled in North and South America, the so-called New World, they relied on enslaved people to grow crops and perform other important tasks. In such places as Brazil and some of the colonies that became the United States, slavery became the foundation of the economy. Few, if any, slaves, however, willingly served their masters. Slaves were property, and masters bought and sold them the way they did food or clothes. Some enslaved people escaped from their masters, knowing they could be punished—or perhaps killed—if they were caught.

In the United States, from the 1830s until the 1860s, the Underground Railroad offered slaves a better chance to find freedom. The Underground Railroad was not a real railroad, and it was not underground. Instead, the Underground Railroad was a series of paths, roads, rivers, and safe houses. Escaped slaves traveled these routes as they fled their masters.

Along the railroad, fleeing slaves, also called runaways or fugitives, relied on help from people who opposed slavery.

Lewis Hayden's house in Boston, Massachusetts, was a prominent station on the Underground Railroad when this picture of him was taken in 1833.

Some of these people were called conductors; they actually took slaves from one house to another on the route north. The houses were called stations or depots, and the people who owned them were called stationmasters. They provided food and shelter for the slaves before they left for the next station.

Some of the people who helped escaping slaves lived along rivers that separated free states and slave states. Others lived in Northern cities where escaped slaves came looking for work or food. Blacks who had been born free or escaped from slavery or otherwise earned their freedom often helped other slaves. At times, American Indian tribes welcomed fleeing slaves. U.S. slaves also found people in the neighboring lands of Mexico and Canada who would protect them and offer them freedom.

FIRST SLAVES, FIRST RUNAWAYS

The story of fugitive slaves and their efforts to find freedom goes back centuries. Most slaves in early times were taken in warfare, but people could become enslaved in other ways.

Some criminals were forced into slavery as punishment for their crimes. People who could not pay their debts often became the slaves of those to whom they owed money, or offered one of their children as a slave. A few people even chose to become slaves, if they had no skills or money. They could at least count on being fed and housed by a master.

From the beginning of slavery, many enslaved people wanted to regain their freedom. Some of the earliest legal documents in existence deal with runaway slaves. In Babylon, a city in ancient Mesopotamia, which was centered in what is now Iraq, King Hammurabi wrote one of the first law codes. The laws said that runaway slaves who were captured could be killed, although most were merely kept in chains. The laws also punished people who helped fugitive slaves: "If a [free-man] has harbored in his house either a fugitive male or female slave . . . and has not brought him forth at the summons of the police, the householder shall be put to death."

Wherever slavery developed, officials tried to deal with enslaved people who ran away. Ancient Rome ordered all runaways to be returned to their masters, leading to the rise of professional slave catchers. These men tracked down slaves to collect rewards.

INTO MODERN TIMES

In 11th-century England, slaves who ran away and were caught were executed. People caught helping runaways had to pay the owners to help cover the cost of the lost "property." During wartime, enslaved people sometimes ran away and joined their masters' enemies. The enemy forces welcomed extra help, and the slaves had the chance to pay back their masters for years of harsh treatment.

Escaped slaves were also a problem in Italian cities of the 14th and 15th centuries. Both city officials and residents joined the hunt for fugitives. In each town, one official would read descriptions of the runaways. Strangers in a town were often caught and questioned. During the questioning, the fugitives might be tortured so officials could learn who had helped them. The Roman Catholic Church, the main church in Italy, helped with the effort to find runaways. The church officials turned in most escaped slaves who tried to hide on church ground.

Starting in the 15th century, European merchants actively sought slaves in Africa. Both Europeans and Africans made money in the slave trade. In the 16th century, the Europeans began taking African slaves to the New World. Historians estimate that about 11 million Africans were taken to the Americas as slaves between 1450 and 1900. Slightly more than 425,000 of them went to British and French colonies in North America. Most ended up in South America and the Caribbean.

The enslaved Africans worked on plantations, large farms that usually produced one main crop sold at markets. Slavery in the Americas eventually led to the first organized effort to help fugitive slaves and, later, to the Underground Railroad itself.

1

Fugitives in the New World

An African slave ship hoists sail in an effort to escape from an English military ship in this woodcut from the 1800s. English ships tried to prevent slave traders from operating along the coast of Africa.

SLAVE TRADERS

In Africa, as in other regions, a person might become a slave after a war or as punishment for a crime. But most African slaves who reached the New World were forced into slavery by slave traders who captured them. Slave traders raided African villages and kidnapped potential slaves. Some raiders were local people who worked with African or European traders.

This woodcut from the 1800s shows a group of Africans kidnapped by armed slave traders being marched to the coast, where they will be sold.

When the slave traders struck, their victims had little time to react. One minute, the villagers were free, living their daily lives with their families. After perhaps a brief struggle, they were overpowered and bound with chains. With that brutal start, the slaves began a journey that took them far from their homes and often cut short their lives. Once under their masters' control, many slaves became fugitives to try to regain their freedom.

Starting in 1502, the Spanish took African slaves to the lands Spain controlled in the New World. These colonies included islands in the Caribbean Sea and parts of South and Central America. After 1519, Mexico was also a part of the Spanish Empire, and some Africans were taken there. The Spanish also enslaved the American Indians they conquered in battle. During the 17th century, the French took some slaves to French territories in Canada, though slavery was never widespread there or in the parts of Canada under English control. Canada lacked the right climate to grow the crops, such as sugar and tobacco, usually raised on plantations.

In 1619, about 20 Africans reached the English colony of Virginia. Historians are unsure if these people were indentured servants or slaves. Many of the first settlers came to America as indentured servants. An indenture was a contract, and an indentured servant agreed to work for a master for up to seven years. In return, the master usually paid for the servant's sea voyage across the Atlantic and supplied food, clothing, and a place to live. When the servant's indenture ended, the master was supposed to provide some money or land to help the servant begin a new life as a free citizen.

Indentured servants could not travel or marry without their master's permission, and some particularly cruel masters beat servants who disobeyed them. Indentured servants, like slaves, sometimes ran away from their masters. In North America, there were indentured servants in many English colonies, although most lived in Virginia and Maryland.

Whether the Africans who first arrived in Virginia were slaves or not, enslaved Africans soon reached New York and Massachusetts. However, in the early years of colonial America, most slaves were American Indians. Landowners also relied on white indentured servants to help run their farms.

FUGITIVES IN ENGLISH COLONIES

After battles with American Indians, the colonists often forced their defeated enemies into slavery. The American colonists soon realized, however, that the Indians were not useful slaves. Males often refused to do farmwork, which was traditionally done by women in Indian society. Indian slaves also found it easy to escape and avoid capture. The Indians knew the countryside better than the settlers did, and others Indians would often shelter them. The colonists found that it made more sense to sell enslaved American Indians to English plantation owners in the West Indies, islands in the Caribbean Sea.

Although the American Indians had an advantage if they tried to escape, colonial leaders still hoped to limit runaways. In 1642, Virginia passed a law that fined anyone who helped a runaway servant. After runaways were caught and returned to their masters, they were branded, or burned with hot metal, in the shape of the letter *R* if they tried a second escape. This law concerning servants hinted at the even harsher laws that lay ahead for slaves. In the decades that followed, officials in the colonies and England passed laws that restricted the actions of slaves. For example, slaves could not leave a plantation without their master's permission. As more laws limited what slaves could do, they had even more reason to try to break free from their masters.

I n 1641, Massachusetts became the first English colony in North America to legalize slavery, though slaves lived in other colonies at that time.

Toward the end of the 17th century, colonists faced a shortage of labor. The pool of Indian slaves had shrunk, partly because of war with the colonists and partly because of disease. The settlers had brought illnesses, such as smallpox and influenza, with them to North America. American Indians had never been exposed to these illnesses before, and large numbers of them died as a result. Landowners did not want to acquire more indentured servants, because they had to keep finding new ones to replace servants whose contracts had ended. In addition, the number of Europeans willing to work as servants in America fell, and their price rose. Buying slaves from Africa seemed the best way to guarantee a steady supply of workers.

The English slaveholders in the West Indies had already seen the value of those enslaved workers. African slaves dominated the workforce on such islands as Jamaica and Barbados. By 1710, for example, Jamaica had 58,000 slaves out of a total population of about 65,000.

AFRICAN FUGITIVES IN THE AMERICAS

From the beginning, African slaves who escaped had a hard time keeping their freedom. White indentured servants who bolted from their masters could blend into a crowd, since most colonies had large white populations. But an unknown African who turned up in a town was automatically assumed to be a slave. As in ancient times, slaves often were branded. People who saw a branded African knew they were probably confronting a slave. Slaves who had just arrived from Africa or the West Indies also faced a language problem, since most of them could not speak English.

Despite the difficulty, some fugitives managed to escape and settled in remote swamplands or mountainous regions. These escaped slaves were called maroons, from a

The first maroon community appeared about 1605 in Brazil, which was a colony of Portugal at that time. Runaway slaves created their own state within the colony. Known as Palmares, this community survived until the end of the 17th century, when Portuguese officials finally destroyed it.

Spanish word meaning "wild" or "savage."

Starting in the early 17th century, some maroons in Brazil and Mexico managed to found their own towns. In the English colonies of North America, about 50 maroon communities managed to survive for a time in the South. The largest maroon town developed in the 18th century in the Great Dismal Swamp, which lies along the border of Virginia and North Carolina. As many as 2,000 people may have lived there.

By 1690, new laws tried to address the problem of fugitive slaves. Connecticut passed a law that year requiring that blacks who were traveling without their masters' permission "shall be stopped and secured by any of the inhabitants." The next year, Virginia passed a law to stop runaway slaves who threatened the safety of free residents. Residents could legally "kill and destroy" these fugitives if they resisted capture after a sheriff issued a call for their arrest.

Starting in the 1690s, African slaves looking to regain their freedom found a friend in the Spanish government. At the time, Spain controlled Florida. Spanish officials feared the

Slave hunters on horseback and their dogs chase an escaped slave through a field.

In 1680, blacks made up about 4.6 percent of the population in England's North American colonies. By 1700, that percentage had nearly tripled, and most of the African Americans in the colonies were slaves.

growing power of the nearby English colonies, especially the Carolinas. The Spanish decided to try to weaken England and boost Florida's population at the same time. In 1693, Spain's king, Carlos II, promised to free any English slaves who escaped to Florida and became Roman Catholics. He said he was "giving liberty to all . . . the men as well as the women . . . so that by their example . . . others will do the same." The freed slaves were later given guns and sent back to the Carolinas to help other slaves escape. Many of these free Africans settled around St. Augustine, Florida. Over the next few decades, they fought bravely for Spain during battles with American Indians and invading English forces from South Carolina.

SLAVERY AND REVOLUTION

During the 18th century, slavery continued to grow in the Americas. Runaways troubled slave owners for two reasons. For one, the owners needed all their slaves to keep their plantations running. Also, since slaves were valuable property, they often made up a large part of a slave owner's wealth. Aside from the maroon villages, however, escaped slaves had few places where they could safely avoid capture. Slavery was legal in all 13 American colonies, and most free people understood their legal duty to help capture and return fugitives.

In April 1775, Massachusetts Patriots and British soldiers fired the first shots of the American Revolution (1775–1783). Most U.S. colonies offered to manumit, or free, slaves if they fought against the British. The British responded by making the same promise to slaves who ran away from their masters if they fought the Americans. In November 1775, John Murray, Lord Dunmore, the British governor of Virginia, offered freedom to both male indentured servants and male slaves who fought the Americans. Like their masters who remained loyal to Great Britain, these slaves were called Loyalists, or Tories. Later in the war, the British said that all slaves, whether they fought or not, would receive their freedom if they escaped from their masters. This offer came as most of the fighting shifted to the South. The British knew how much the Southern economy relied on the hard work of the region's slaves.

Fugitives and American Indians

Across the colonies, some fugitive slaves found help from American Indians. At times, former slaves and Indians married and started families. Some of the Indians were survivors of outbreaks of disease or war with the English. Taking in fugitives helped the remaining Indians keep their tribes alive. During the 18th century, large numbers of slaves found safety with the Creek of Georgia and the Seminole of Florida.

By one estimate, tens of thousands of African-American slaves left the plantations to join the British. Not surprisingly, American owners tried to prevent their slaves from running away. South Carolina officials searched ships before they left port, to make sure no fugitive slaves were hiding on board. That state also threatened to kill any escaped slave who was caught, and it did execute a free black named Jerry who tried to help slaves escape and join the British.

Disease as a Weapon

British general Alexander Leslie had a gruesome use for some of the escaped slaves who fought alongside his men. Hundreds of the African Americans had smallpox, a deadly disease that easily passes from one person to another. The general wrote, "I shall distribute them about the rebel plantations." The general hoped the slaves would spread their smallpox to the Americans. This incident was an early example of germ or biological warfare, which involves spreading a disease to weaken an enemy.

When the American Revolution ended in 1783, the British upset U.S. leaders by refusing to give back some runaways who had earned their freedom by fighting for Great Britain. Sir Guy Carleton, the British commander in the United States, said that giving back the runaways would be "a dishonorable violation of the public faith." But the British also kept some of the runaways as slaves and took them to other British colonies after the war. For the hundreds of thousands of slaves who stayed with their masters, the war did not change their situation. U.S. leaders said the American Revolution had been fought to defend liberty, but that personal freedom rarely applied to slaves.

2

A New Country
and Its Slaves

With his arm outstretched, John Nixon reads the Declaration of Independence
to people gathered in front of the State House in Philadelphia, Pennsylvania,
immediately after the document's passage. The Declaration promised freedom
for many Americans, but it did not abolish slavery.

CHANGING ATTITUDES

With the Declaration of Independence in 1776, the 13 British colonies in North America created a new country—the United States. The U.S. victory over the British in the American Revolution guaranteed the new nation's independence. During the war, slavery was legal in every state. Few white Americans at the time were concerned about ending slavery or helping individual slaves win their freedom.

George Washington is shown with some of the slaves he owned working in the fields on his farm. Some of the founders of the United States, such as Washington and Thomas Jefferson, owned slaves while others, such as Benjamin Franklin, opposed slavery.

When the war ended, many Northern states began a gradual process of ending slavery. Children of slaves would gain their freedom when they reached adulthood. In 1783, a Massachusetts court said slavery was illegal, making that state the first of the original 13 to ban slavery completely.

The changing attitude toward slavery in the North benefited Southern runaways. If they could reach a "free" state, they had a better chance of keeping their freedom. Fugitives often changed their names, making it harder for owners to track them down. The fugitives might live with free blacks in such major cities as Philadelphia, Pennsylvania; Boston, Massachusetts; and New York City.

Many African Americans who had already won their freedom believed they had a duty to help and protect runaways. Their efforts included hiding the slaves, giving them food and clothing, and helping them find jobs. These efforts by free blacks were later duplicated by whites who worked on the Underground Railroad.

Even before the American Revolution, some prominent citizens in Philadelphia wanted to aid enslaved African Americans. These citizens were Quakers, members of a religious group known as the Society of Friends. The Quakers thought that all people were equal under God. This belief led to their strong feelings against slavery. In 1775, some Philadelphia Quakers formed the first major antislavery group, the Society for the Relief of Free Negroes Unlawfully Held in Bondage. After the Revolution, the society's members included some well-known non-Quakers, including Benjamin Franklin and Noah Webster. The society wanted both to end slavery and to improve the lives of blacks who were already free. Members of other Protestant faiths, particularly Congregationalists, Methodists, and Baptists, also aided slaves.

FUGITIVES AND THE LAW

In 1787, the 13 states held a convention in Philadelphia. Its goal was to strengthen the national government. The government that Congress had created during the American Revolution lacked several key powers. For example, it could not effectively settle disputes between the states or force the states to pay taxes to the federal government. The delegates at the Philadelphia convention created the U.S.

Constitution. This document outlined how the new government would function. It also spelled out certain basic laws. The Constitution remains today the foundation of the U.S. government.

At the Constitutional Convention, the delegates hotly debated slavery. Southerners opposed any effort to limit slavery. In the end, they accepted the idea of limiting the slave trade after 1807. This meant that slave traders could not bring in new slaves from outside the country, although slaves could still be bought and sold within the United States.

Another part of the Constitution said that three-fifths of all slaves would be counted when figuring a state's population. So, for example, 100 slaves would be counted as 60 people. Northerners had not wanted slaves counted at all. A state's population determines how many members it sends to the House of Representatives, which helps write the country's laws. Since slaves could not vote, Northerners thought they should not count in the formula for setting the number of representatives. The North did not want slaves to give Southern states a larger share of the representatives in the House. Some Southern states, however, had a much larger percentage of slaves than white residents. Those states wanted slaves counted to make sure that the states had as many representatives as Northern states. Counting just three-fifths of all enslaved people was a compromise between the North and South.

The Constitution also addressed the issue of fugitive slaves. The Constitution recognized the right of slave owners to reclaim their runaway slaves, saying that a free state could not pass laws that helped escaped slaves keep their freedom.

While the Constitutional Convention was under way, Congress also took other actions that affected slaves and runaways. In July 1787, the lawmakers passed the Northwest Ordinance. This law dealt with U.S. lands east of the Mississippi River and north of the Ohio River, called the Northwest Territory. This region was eventually split into the states of Ohio, Indiana, Illinois, Wisconsin, and Michigan. A part of Minnesota was also in the territory. The Northwest Ordinance outlawed slavery in the region, although masters living there who already owned slaves could keep them. Slaves who fled to the Northwest Territory and were caught had to be returned to their masters.

During the 1780s, escaped slaves presented a diplomatic problem for the young United States. As they had during colonial times, some enslaved African Americans escaped to Florida, which was still under Spanish control. The old Spanish offer of freedom to fugitives still applied. Slave owners in the South, especially Georgia and the Carolinas, protested this Spanish policy, which encouraged slaves to escape. Rather than risk bad relations with the United States, Spain finally agreed to end its policy of granting freedom to fugitives in 1790, though the African Americans already there remained free.

With slavery illegal in the Northwest Territory, some Canadian slaves fled from their masters and headed south into the United States. In at least one instance, a U.S. court ruled that the fugitives could stay in the United States.

The first U.S. Census, taken in 1790, showed that the United States had just over 757,000 African Americans—about 19 percent of the total population. Almost 700,000 of them were slaves. Just four states—Virginia, South Carolina, North Carolina, and Maryland—had slightly more than 600,000 of these enslaved people.

THE FIRST FUGITIVE SLAVE ACT

The Constitution called for returning escaped slaves to their masters, but it did not deal with the specifics of catching runaways. In 1793, Congress addressed that issue with the country's first fugitive slave act. Under the law, anyone caught aiding an escaped slave faced a $500 fine. The Fugitive Slave Act of 1793 allowed slave owners or people working for them to track down enslaved people who ran for freedom. The slave owners then took the fugitives they caught to a local judge or government official. The fugitives had to prove that they were not slaves. Since judges were more likely to believe white slave owners and slave catchers than African Americans, some free blacks actually lost their freedom after the new law was passed. Some slave catchers kidnapped free African Americans in the North. The slave catchers counted on the courts' ignoring any evidence that the "slaves" might actually be free.

In 1799, a group of free African Americans in Philadelphia asked Congress to take action, since blacks were being "hunted by armed Men, and . . . cruelly treated, shot, or brought back in chains to those who have no just claim upon them." Congress ignored the call to change the Fugitive Slave Act or prevent the kidnappings.

FIFTY DOLLARS REWARD.

Ran away from Mount Welby, Prince George's County, Maryland, on Monday, the 2d inst., a negro man calling himself Joe Bond, about 25 years of age, about 5 feet 6 inchesin height, stout built, copper complexion; the only mark recollected is a peculiar speck in one of his eyes. Had on when he went away a frock tweed coat, dark brown, and cap near the

This handbill from 1850 is typical of the detailed descriptions of runaway slaves that were posted by slave hunters. A reward of $50 would be equivalent to more than $1,000 today.

The same year that Congress passed the Fugitive Slave Act, a new invention was introduced in the South. The cotton gin made it easy to remove the seeds in cotton. With the machine, farm workers could clean 50 times more cotton per day than by hand. Farmers in some Southern states quickly began planting more cotton, leading to a higher demand for slaves to work in the fields and clean the cotton. Sugar and rice were two other important crops grown on new plantations developing in the South. More than ever, the region's economy was tied to the labor of enslaved people.

O ne well-known free black in Philadelphia who faced kidnapping was Richard Allen. A minister, Allen helped found the Free African Society and the African Methodist Episcopal Church (AME). The AME was the first independent Protestant church for African Americans. Allen had been free for 20 years when a slave catcher accused him of being a runaway. Allen went to court and successfully defended his status as a free man. Allen and members of his church helped fugitive slaves who reached Philadelphia, forming a part of the Underground Railroad before it was even named. Slaves sometimes hid in the church or in Allen's home.

WHO ESCAPED—AND WHY?

At the beginning of the 19th century, fugitives were a problem for most Southern slave owners. At one time or another, almost all of them had at least one slave who fled. Some slaves left for just a short period, perhaps to take a break from work or to visit relatives on another plantation. Other enslaved people hoped to escape for good, for a variety of reasons.

One of the enslaved African Americans who fled to Florida was Prince Witten. In 1786, Witten, his wife, and their two children escaped from their Georgia master. An ad seeking their return said, "It is supposed that Prince has carried them with him to Florida to avoid separation from his family . . . to which he is much attached." In Florida, Witten settled in St. Augustine and worked as a carpenter. In 1795, he asked the governor of Florida to give him land, and the governor agreed. Witten eventually became one of the wealthiest African Americans in the colony.

Slaves did not like being separated from their families or dealing with mean masters. Many slaves also ran away to escape punishment after they committed crimes. Escaping could also be a way to get out of a bad marriage or avoid other family problems. For many fugitives, however, the desire to be free was reason enough to run.

Slaves who made the decision to escape showed tremendous courage, given the odds against their avoiding capture and punishment. Some runaways could not find food, and their hunger forced them back to their masters. Others ran away again and again, despite the punishments they faced when they were caught. Some enslaved African Americans who ran away many times turned violent in their quest for freedom. In 1805, one Virginia slave owner warned others that "great care should be taken to secure" his runaway slave: "I expect he is desperate as well as vicious." Laws and slave catchers could not stop slaves who were determined to seek freedom.

3

The Railroad Takes Shape

The house of Elizabeth Buffum Chace in Valley Falls, Rhode Island, was an Underground Railroad station. Runaway slaves were sheltered here as they made their way to freedom in the North and in Canada.

THE WAR OF 1812

In 1812, the United States fought Great Britain a second time. U.S. leaders believed British naval policies were harmful to the country. The British tried to restrict U.S. trade and at times forced Americans to serve on British warships, a practice called impressment. During the War of 1812, the British and Americans fought both on land and at sea.

A group of British sailors capture an American in Boston shortly before the War of 1812. Captured Americans were forced to serve in the British navy.

As they had in the American Revolution, the British encouraged enslaved African Americans to desert their masters. In 1813, a shipload of runaway slaves reached Nova Scotia, Canada, where many African-American Loyalists had settled after the American Revolution. The next year, a British admiral recruited U.S. slaves to fight for the British. Several thousand accepted this offer, and fugitive slaves fought U.S. troops at the Battle of New Orleans in Louisiana, the last major conflict of the war. John Quincy Adams was one of the Americans who signed the treaty that ended the war. He noted in a letter that "the British naval Commanders . . . have carried away from the United States all the slaves they have taken." The British eventually paid Southern slave owners just over $1 million to cover the loss of their slaves.

In 1793, lawmakers in Upper Canada—what is now Ontario—ended the slave trade there. They also called for the gradual emancipation, or freeing, of slaves. After the American Revolution, several thousands slaves who fought for the British and were granted their freedom went to Canada. Many of them settled in Nova Scotia. This migration greatly increased the number of free blacks in Canada. The War of 1812 created another group of freed slaves in Canada. Gradually, American slaves learned that Canada was a desirable place to live, if they could escape and safely reach the border.

INDIAN WARS

Reaching Canada was a goal for some escaped slaves, but even when the Underground Railroad was fully developed, the trip north was too long and dangerous for slaves from the Deep South. This part of the United States is usually considered to include Alabama, Arkansas, Florida, Georgia, Louisiana, Mississippi, Texas, and parts of the Carolinas and Tennessee. If Canada was too far, many slaves headed to East Florida, which was still under Spanish control. (The smaller region of West Florida became part of the United States in 1803.)

American Indians of the Seminole tribe lived in the central part of East Florida. The Seminole, like white Americans, practiced slavery, but they gave their slaves much more freedom. Runaway African-American slaves who went to Seminole lands were allowed to live in their own communities. In effect, the Indians treated them as free people, even though the African Americans were technically slaves. Over time, the fugitives learned the Seminole language and adopted some of their culture. Many Indians and African Americans married, creating what is now considered a distinct cultural group, the black Seminole.

The word *Seminole* comes from a Spanish word meaning "fugitive." The Seminole Indians were originally members of the Creek tribe who left to live on their own. The word *maroon* shares the same Spanish root as Seminole.

To Southern slave owners, the Seminole and the independent black towns were a threat. As long as they existed, slaves would be tempted to flee to Florida. Conflict between the United States and the Seminole grew after the War of 1812. Americans accused the Indians and the fugitive slaves of raiding U.S. communities. To stop the raids, General Andrew Jackson invaded Florida in 1818. Jackson, who would be elected U.S. president in 1828, saw defeating the Seminole and the fugitives as part of a larger effort to win Florida from Spain. He believed that Florida would be payment for "the outrages of Spain upon the Property of our Citizens"—in other words, Spain's protection of runaway slaves.

Jackson's invasion was a success: He defeated the Spanish, and East Florida became part of the United States in 1819. The Seminole, however, continued to live in the swamps of Florida, with free blacks nearby, and Southern slaves continued to seek their freedom by joining the Seminole. The existence of Seminole and fugitive slave communities eventually led to more fighting between the United States and the Seminole. In the end, after 1842, U.S. troops forced most Seminole to move to reservations in Oklahoma. U.S. officials granted freedom to fugitive African Americans who went with the Indians.

CROSSING THE OHIO

For Southern slaves who did head north, one of the early, important routes crossed the Ohio River. If fugitives successfully made it across, the river slowed down any pursuing slave catchers. North of the Ohio River were Illinois, Indiana, and Ohio. By 1818, each was a free state, where slavery was not allowed. Of the three, Ohio played the largest role in the development of the Underground Railroad.

The River of Freedom

To many runaway slaves, the Ohio River was known as the River Jordan. This name referred to the Bible story of the Israelites, who had been slaves in Egypt. They had to cross the Jordan River to reach Israel, the land God had promised to them. For enslaved African Americans, Ohio and other states north of the Ohio River were their "Promised Land," where they would have their freedom.

Ohio was the first state from the Old Northwest Territories to join the Union (in 1803). Free blacks and Quakers settled in Ohio. So did a variety of abolitionists—people who wanted the immediate abolition, or end, of slavery. The free blacks and antislavery whites of Ohio were eager to help enslaved people win their freedom. The state bordered two slave states, Kentucky and Virginia. (In 1863 the area of Virginia that borders Ohio became a separate state, West Virginia.)

Ohio also had a long shoreline along Lake Erie. Fugitives who wanted to go to Canada could travel overland or sail across the lake into Ontario. Other runaways headed to states north and west of Ohio, to get as far away as possible from their old masters and the slave catchers.

Slaves who became Christians often used Bible stories to explain their own situation and their hope for a better life. Famous conductors on the Underground Railroad, such as Harriet Tubman, were called "Moses." In the Bible, Moses was the Jewish prophet who led the Israelites out of their slavery in Egypt.

In Ohio, informal efforts to help runaway slaves began as early as 1815. The state's importance to fugitives grew as soldiers returning from the War of 1812 talked about the free land that sat across the Ohio River. Some slaves who heard these tales made the decision to cross the river and head north. By 1817, Kentucky slave owners were beginning to grumble about the number of slaves crossing the Ohio.

Some runaways received help from free blacks living in Ohio. A community of Virginia slaves who had become free after their masters died settled along the Ohio River near the town of Ripley. This and other black communities provided shelter to enslaved people. Other free African Americans settled in port cities and towns, such as Cincinnati, Ohio. At times, the free blacks in Cincinnati persuaded slaves traveling through the city with their masters to bolt for freedom.

EARLY LEADERS OF THE OHIO RAILROAD

One of the most important figures in Ohio's Underground Railroad was John Rankin. A white Presbyterian minister who strongly opposed slavery, Rankin settled in Ripley, Ohio, in 1822. The village sat along the banks of the Ohio River. Rankin soon began helping fugitives who crossed the Ohio. He hid them in his barn until he could arrange to take them to other people farther into Ohio who were equally eager to help the runaways escape.

In 1828, Rankin and his family moved to a new house in Ripley. It sat on a hill overlooking the river. In the front yard stood a flagpole. At night, Rankin used the pole to hang a lantern whose light could be seen across the river in

Reverend John Rankin's safe house in Ripley, Ohio, was situated on a hill that made it easy for runaways to spot as they crossed the Ohio River from the slave state of Kentucky.

Kentucky. As one former slave said, the lantern "always meant freedom for the slave if he could get to this light."

Rankin's bold decision to hang out this light proudly displayed his efforts to help fugitives. He sometimes faced mobs of angry slave owners from Kentucky. Rankin and his son beat off their attackers and continued their work. During his career, Rankin helped as many as 2,000 people escape from slavery.

At times Rankin worked with a former slave named John Parker, who had bought his own freedom and settled in Cincinnati. Parker owned a business, and he gave some of the money he made to fund the Underground Railroad in Ripley. Parker was also one of the few members of the railroad who dared travel into the South and bring slaves back north with him. He once said that runaways were "usually strong physically, as well as people of character, and were resourceful when confronted with trouble, other wise they never would have escaped."

Another white Southerner who moved north and helped fugitives was the Quaker Levi Coffin. In 1826, he and his wife Catherine moved to Newport (now Fountain City), Indiana, to open a store. They found that free blacks in the area were helping fugitives, and they joined the effort. The Coffins offered food, clothing, and a place to sleep. Their activities upset proslavery neighbors, who stopped buying goods at the Coffins' store. Still, the Coffins continued their work on the Underground Railroad.

Other Welcoming Stops

Many residents in Indiana and Illinois played important roles in the early days of the Underground Railroad, though these states had fewer centers of activity than Ohio. In Madison, Indiana, free blacks led the effort to help fugitives. Charles Blockson, a historian of the Underground Railroad, says a large number of slaves crossed the Ohio River in Indiana because spots along the river offered good hiding places. Slaves entered Illinois by crossing both the Ohio and Mississippi Rivers at a number of points. In Indiana or Illinois, the workers on the Underground Railroad often sent fugitives northward to Chicago, Illinois, or on to Canada.

Levi Coffin's efforts increased when his family moved to Cincinnati in the 1840s. Like Rankin, Coffin did not hide his work helping slaves, and at one point, he was called "the president of the Underground Railroad." That name, however, hides the true nature of the railroad. It was not one large system, but a network of small systems that often overlapped. No one person was ever in charge of the railroad.

Before crossing the Ohio River, many fugitives received help from people in Kentucky or other parts of the South, both white and black. Some Southern whites would aid runaways for a fee. They would hide the slaves in wagons or on boats. Free friends and relatives often saved money to help them pay for their escape. Coffin wrote in his autobiography, "I have always contended that the Underground Railroad, so called, was a Southern institution; that it had its origin in the Slave states."

When Coffin reached Cincinnati, the city already had a thriving system to help runaways in place. Most members of the early railroad in the city were African Americans. Henry Boyd was one of the first free blacks to settle in Cincinnati and help enslaved African Americans find freedom. Boyd had once tried to run away himself, before finally buying his freedom. According to one abolitionist who visited Cincinnati, Boyd's home there—not Coffin's—was the first stop for runaways.

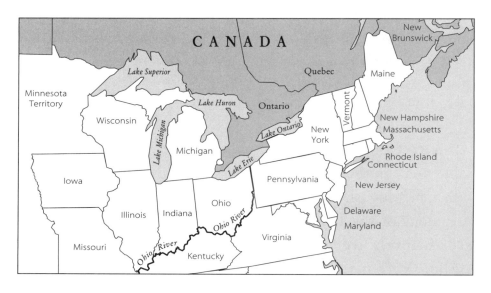

Escaping slaves crossed the Ohio River from Virginia and Kentucky into free states of the North on their way to Canada.

SLAVE REVOLTS AND RUNAWAYS

Having enslaved workers run off was a problem for slave owners, but it did not pose a danger. Slave revolts, on the other hand, could be deadly for any whites in the path of the rebels. Since colonial days, slave owners and lawmakers had tried to limit the number of slaves who could meet in one place. Whites also tried to prevent slaves from having guns. Despite those efforts, slaves sometimes banded together to attack their masters and whites in general.

By their nature, armed revolts were some slaves' attempts to win their freedom. At least one rebellion started out as a mass escape. In 1739, slaves near Stono, South Carolina, rebelled so they could flee to Spanish Florida. The enslaved blacks stole weapons and supplies before heading south. On their way to Florida, they encouraged more slaves to join them and killed about 25 whites. A large group of armed whites finally ended the rebellion before the slaves reached Florida.

In the 1820s and 1830s, two slave revolts—one real and one merely a plan—stirred fear among Southern whites. Denmark Vesey was a free black living in Charleston, South Carolina. In 1822, he supposedly organized a plot to end slavery in the city. Word of the revolt leaked out, and Vesey was arrested and executed with numerous others.

Almost 10 years later, Nat Turner convinced some fellow slaves to rebel against their masters. Soon, Turner was commanding a rebel army that grew as the slaves moved across the Virginia countryside. About 60 whites were killed. Virginia residents struck back by killing and torturing any slaves they could find, whether they had joined the revolt or not. Turner, like Vesey, was eventually caught, tried, and executed, along with 23 other enslaved people. Numerous other blacks were lynched, or murdered by a mob of whites.

Nat Turner's rebellion led to stronger law enforcement in some free states. Ohio and other states bordering the South started enforcing existing laws that limited the arrival of free blacks. Before the rebellion, these laws were often ignored. Now, white residents of these states feared the growing black population.

Slave revolts, particularly Turner's, made life even more difficult for African Americans in the South, both slave and free. Southern politicians demanded tougher laws to limit the activities of blacks. After Turner's revolt, some Southern states passed laws preventing African-American ministers from speaking in public. The whites feared that religious meetings gave blacks a chance to plan revolts. Other laws made it a crime to teach slaves how to read or write. Some states passed laws that prohibited blacks from meeting anywhere in public, and Delaware ruled that free blacks could not own guns.

The slave revolts weakened the efforts of the few Southern abolitionists to win support for ending slavery. Now more Southern whites argued for preserving slavery at all costs. The new laws and the increased effort to preserve slavery in the South led more slaves to consider escaping and more abolitionists to help them. The most active years of the Underground Railroad were about to begin.

4

The Railroad Gains Steam

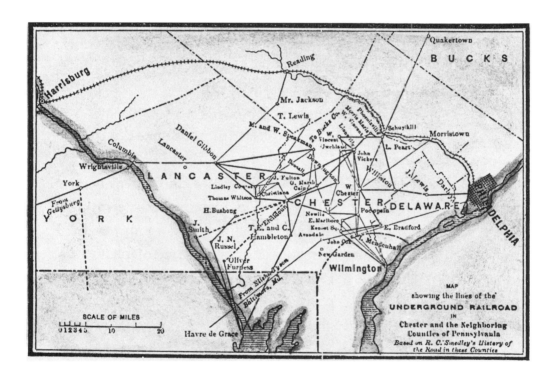

This 19th-century map shows the routes traveled by fugitives on the
Underground Railroad in part of Pennsylvania near Philadelphia.
Pennsylvania was a free state that bordered the slave states of Maryland
and Virginia and was the home of many abolitionist Quakers.

NAMING THE UNDERGROUND RAILROAD

For years, individual blacks and whites on both sides of the Mason-Dixon line had been helping fugitives escape from slavery. (The Mason-Dixon line, first drawn as the southern boundary of Pennsylvania, referred to the informal border between free states and slave states.) By 1831, a loose system was already linking the rescuers together in some areas, such as the Ohio River valley. However, the name *Underground Railroad* still did not exist. Several different stories suggest how the railroad received its name. All reflect the fact that real railroads were an exciting new form of transportation at the time—the first train service in the United States began in 1828. The name *Underground Railroad* also hinted at the secrecy required to bring enslaved people from the South into free states and Canada.

The earliest story explaining how the railroad was named dates to 1831. A slave named Tice Davids fled Kentucky, swam across the Ohio River, and slipped away somewhere near Sandusky, Ohio. His master was unable to locate him and supposedly said that Davids "must have gone off on an underground road." According to a similar account, this incident took place near Columbia, Pennsylvania. Another possible source for the name was a Washington, D.C., newspaper storythat supposedly described a fugitive slave who was captured and tortured. He told officials that he had planned to head north, using a "railroad that went underground all the way to Boston." One historian who researched 19th-century newspapers found that the earliest mention of the Underground Railroad occurred in New York in 1842.

This page from the 1844 diary of Daniel Osborn, an Ohio Quaker, records the fugitives he aided during a five-month period.

THE ABOLITIONIST MOVEMENT AND RUNAWAYS

Whenever the name *Underground Railroad* first appeared, the idea of a secret system that helped slaves escape soon spread. Abolitionists suggested that the railroad was a highly developed, formal network. They hoped to win support by showing Americans the dangers slaves risked when they ran for their freedom. Some freed slaves spoke at public meetings, describing their lives as slaves and their journey north. Abolitionists hoped that these stories would convince other

Northerners to support the end of slavery. At one meeting in Ohio, an entire fugitive family addressed the audience. An observer noted, "Many eyes were filled with tears."

Advertising the Railroad

Historians in the past once talked about the secret nature of the Underground Railroad. Some people who helped fugitives did keep their activities quiet, especially if they were hiding runaways, but in some locations, the conductors and stationmasters acted openly. A few members of the railroad even took out newspaper ads to promote their activities. In 1844, an Illinois paper ran an ad saying that "the U.R.R. [Underground Railroad] is in excellent order. The station keepers . . . are all active and trustworthy men, [and slaves] intrusted to their care will be forwarded with great care." Another ad promised fugitives "trains fitted up in the best style of accommodations for passengers" on their way to "Libertyville, Upper Canada." The ad called the railroad the "Liberty Line."

Starting in the 1830s, abolitionists formed the first national organizations committed to ending slavery. In 1832, William Lloyd Garrison helped found the American Anti-Slavery Society. State and local antislavery societies quickly appeared throughout the North. As abolitionism spread, more whites took an interest in helping runaway slaves. One abolitionist of the 1830s who was active in the Underground Railroad was Gerrit Smith. A wealthy landowner, Smith lived in upstate New York, close to Lake Ontario. Smith hid fugitive slaves in his home until he could arrange for them to take a boat across the lake into Canada. One time, Smith sent a young girl named Harriet across the lake just hours before her master came looking for her. When Smith learned that she had reached Canada, he published a letter to the master in a local paper. Teasing the master, Smith wrote that the man "would no doubt rejoice to know that his slave Harriet, in whose fate he felt so deep an interest, was now a free woman."

Black abolitionists often played a part in the Underground Railroad through groups called vigilance committees. The committees promoted the abolition of slavery and aided runaways. The best known of these groups was probably the Philadelphia Vigilance Committee. Founded in 1835, it included both black and white abolitionists. Over time, however, free blacks dominated the group's leadership. Philadelphia was close to the slave states of Maryland and Delaware. Enslaved people escaping on foot had a good chance of reaching Philadelphia. The city also had a thriving port, so some runaways hid on ships heading there.

The Philadelphia Vigilance Committee gave fugitives money, medical aid, food, and a place to stay before helping them reach New England or Canada. Committee members also advised runaways in legal battles against slave catchers. One key member was Robert Purvis, who was sometimes called "the president of the Underground Railroad" in Pennsylvania. Purvis, a free African American, served for a time as president of the Philadelphia Vigilance Committee.

Many abolitionists remained active in the Underground Railroad throughout the Civil War and aided fugitives any way they could. One of their most daring methods was "slave stealing." In a reverse of the kidnapping of free blacks in the North, these abolitionists went into the South and took

Robert Purvis was born in Charleston, South Carolina, in 1810. He was the son of a white man and a free African-American woman. Purvis came to Philadelphia in 1819. In college there, he met William Lloyd Garrison and helped Garrison found the American Anti-Slavery Society. While serving on the Philadelphia Vigilance Committee, Purvis often held meetings in his home to plot how to help runaways. Purvis's house also had a trap door that led to a secret room where fugitives hid from slave catchers.

slaves off their plantations. Abolitionists who helped enslaved people this way risked arrest and even death.

In 1844, a Massachusetts sea captain named Jonathan Walker was arrested in Florida. Local officials branded him with *SS*, for "slave stealer," and then sent him to jail for several months. Two years later, an abolitionist named John Greenleaf Whittier wrote a poem about Walker and his attempt to help runaways. In "The Branded Hand," Whittier wrote, "Then lift that manly right hand, bold ploughman of the wave! / Its branded palm shall prophesy, 'Salvation to the Slave!'"

Not all slave stealers helped Southern slaves. Some people just pretended to be slave stealers but were really slave catchers. They promised to put slaves on the Underground Railroad but then kidnapped the slaves and sold them in another part of the South.

INTO THE DEEP SOUTH

The changing nature of slavery during the 1830s and 1840s increased the number of fugitives. Since the early 1800s, Americans had been pushing farther west across North America. Southern farmers moved from the regions close to the Atlantic Ocean farther inland and into the Deep South. Some parts of this region became U.S. territory with the Louisiana Purchase of 1803. The United States doubled in size by adding this land, which it bought from France. Texas later became part of the Deep South when it entered the Union in 1845.

The expansion westward stirred strong debate over the spread of slavery in the United States. Southerners did not want a repeat of the Northwest Ordinance of 1787, which prohibited slavery in the Northwest Territory. Many Northerners, however, did not want to expand slavery. Eventually, slave territories would become slave states, which would send proslavery lawmakers to Congress. Northern politicians feared that proslavery forces would start to dominate the country's policies. In 1820, a series of actions by Congress called the Missouri Compromise supposedly ended the debate. Slavery would be allowed only in new territories south of Missouri's southern border. Missouri itself entered the Union as a slave state.

In the Deep South, plantations producing sugar, rice, and especially cotton quickly spread. The growth of these farms led to a large increase in slavery. In 1810, the United States had about 1.2 million slaves, mostly in the Upper South. By 1840, the number had more than doubled. According to the Constitution, importing slaves into the country was illegal after 1808, although some slave traders avoided the law by smuggling. The new plantations of the Deep South received most of their slaves from the older slave regions of Maryland, Virginia, and the Carolinas. Between 1790 and 1860, approximately 350,000 to 500,000 slaves made the journey westward, sold from one master to another.

This slave trade within the United States devastated slaves. Slave traders split up husbands and wives, parents and children, brothers and sisters. The members of many slave families already lived apart, in different towns or on different plantations, but still fairly close to their relatives. They could usually find a way to see their wives or husbands and children. If one family member were sold to a new master hundreds of miles away, however, the odds of reuniting were small. Rather than risk being sold to new owners and separated from their relatives, enslaved people sometimes ran away.

If they could not escape before being sold, some slaves ran away while they were being transported or once they reached their new masters. One trader placed an ad in a Virginia paper for two runaways. He wrote, "They were purchased by me for the purpose of trading," and he was sure that the two men would try "to reach their former homes."

A large number of fugitives fled from the Deep South back to the coast, near friends and relatives. Most were husbands or wives seeking their partners. Men were more likely to travel long distances and to make repeated attempts if they were caught. A slave named Thomas Taylor tried four times in one year to return to his wife in Mississippi after being sold down the river to New Orleans. A small number of children also ran away, hoping to return to their parents.

SOUTH TO FREEDOM

After 1829, slaves in the Deep South could find their freedom in Mexico. In September of that year, the Mexican government abolished slavery. Even before this, Southern slaves had found freedom in Texas and neighboring lands that were then still part of Mexico. As they did in the South, some fugitives stayed with American Indian tribes. In 1835, an American visitor to south Texas met a Comanche who spoke English. The Indian called the language "the slave tongue," suggesting that he had learned it from a runaway slave. The Comanche added, "In every clan will be found a few who can speak it."

The runaway slave in this 19th-century wood engraving is wearing a slave collar with bells so his master can hear his movements.

The abolition of slavery in Mexico angered the American Texans, who were sometimes called Texians. When the Texians protested, the Mexican government said that slavery could still exist in Texas. A year later, however, the Mexican

government placed new restrictions on bringing slaves into the region.

The Texians did not like the limits on the slave trade. They also were angry that their slaves could win their freedom if they reached Mexico. The slavery issue was just one reason why Texians and Mexicans living in Texas launched a revolution in 1836. After a short war with Mexico, Texas became an independent country, though with close ties to the United States. Some slaves in Texas used the chaos of the war to flee their masters. At least a few joined the Mexican army and fought the rebels. Some Mexican military officers, however, returned fleeing slaves to their masters.

Once Texas won its independence, it made slavery and the slave trade legal and restricted the freedom of free blacks. Few Southern slaves sought their freedom there. They continued on to Mexico, joining the fugitive slaves from Texas who fled there. Mexico, like Canada, offered the promise of a better life. To Texas slave owners, Mexico was a threat, since the government would not return enslaved African Americans who settled there.

5

Riding the Railroad

Slaves traveled north with only the belongings they could carry as they made their way along the Underground Railroad in 1838. They often traveled hundreds of miles on foot to reach free states in the North or the Canadian border.

TRAVELING ON THE UNDERGROUND RAILROAD

By the time the Underground Railroad was named, only a few older African Americans were still held as slaves in the northern United States. Southern slaves were the main "riders" served by the Underground Railroad.

The first step was making the decision to flee. Most often the fugitive was a lone male. A Northern abolitionist wrote that each fugitive "deserves . . . our praise for the skill with which he contrived his escape, and the courage with which he accomplished it." The Christmas season was a popular time to escape. During that time of year, masters often gave enslaved workers permission to visit relatives on nearby plantations. The slaves carried special passes that allowed them to travel. Whites would not have been surprised to see one or two slaves walking on a country road. Some fugitives ran off without passes, hoping they would not be caught. Others stole passes or created forgeries that looked like real passes.

Before leaving, the runaways gathered what food they could. Most traveled very lightly, with little more than the clothes they wore. Once on the road, they sometimes stole food from farms or received food from African Americans they met along the way. William Wells Brown wrote about stealing and eating ears of corn: "During the next day, while in the woods, I roasted my corn and feasted upon it."

Fugitives sought shelter in barns or simply slept in fields or forests, usually during the day. They traveled by night, when they would be harder to detect. Many enslaved people never heard about the Underground Railroad before they made their escape. Sheer luck put them in contact with free blacks or friendly whites who knew where the slaves could receive help on their journey north.

This illustration was published in 1872 in a book about the Underground Railroad that claimed to be an authentic account of the hardships and "death-struggles" of those who traveled it. An escaped slave is shown hiding in a tree to avoid capture.

THE SOUTHERN RAILROAD

Although they often had to rely on their own survival skills, some fugitive slaves in the South did come in contact with the Underground Railroad. North Carolina had a small community of Quakers, who often aided runaways. Whites in the state who opposed slavery brought fugitives food, hid them from slave catchers, and at times loaned them horses. Maryland was an important crossing point for slaves heading north. In the western part of the state, fugitives crossed the Appalachian Mountains into Pennsylvania. In the Eastern Shore region, along the Chesapeake Bay, they sailed small boats up the Susquehanna River into Pennsylvania. In Virginia, slaves often headed for several towns near the Ohio River, including Parkersburg (which is now part of West Virginia).

Delaware was unique among the slave states. Under its laws, blacks were considered free unless someone could prove in court that they were slaves. The state had a large population of free blacks and a strong abolitionist movement. Yet it also had slave owners who resisted any effort to end slavery. As in Maryland, fugitives could take water routes from Delaware into Pennsylvania. They could also travel by land into New Jersey.

One of the most notable conductors on the Underground Railroad was Thomas Garrett of Wilmington, Delaware. Garrett, a white Quaker, claimed to have helped more than 2,000 enslaved African Americans reach the North. He often worked with Quakers who lived nearby in Pennsylvania. He also worked closely with free blacks from his home state, including Samuel Burris and Abraham Shadd. Burris sometimes took fleeing slaves across the Delaware River into Pennsylvania. On one trip, Burris was caught and almost sold into slavery. An abolitionist friend saved him by pretending to be a slave trader and outbidding the other traders seeking to buy Burris.

One Virginia slave who found the Underground Railroad was Charles Peyton Lucas. Around 1850, he and two enslaved friends sneaked off and headed north. For 10 days, they traveled through the countryside, their stomachs often aching for food. Finally, desperate for help, Lucas and his friends stopped at a farmhouse. The farmer, realizing that the slaves were fugitives, gave them directions so they could keep moving and avoid being captured. He also told them where to find other people who could help them on their journey. Sure enough, the slaves followed the farmer's route and met a family that fed them. The wife told them where to go next. "Soon," Lucas wrote, "we struck the track of the underground railroad." Lucas eventually reached Canada.

ESCAPING BY SEA

Since colonial times, Southern ship owners had used enslaved sailors on their vessels. Sailing from one port to another, these sailors had many chances to jump ship and find their freedom. Free and enslaved black sailors also helped other slaves escape, hiding them on their vessels. Some fugitives passed themselves off as free men and found jobs on ships that took them far from their pursuing masters.

The large number of African-American sailors, shipbuilders, and dockworkers also attracted runaways to the port cities of the South. Fugitives knew that the black populations in those cities could at least offer them aid, if not passage north. With luck, the runaways might also find white captains willing to help them because they opposed slavery—or because the slaves had money. Acting on their own, some slaves looking for freedom sneaked onto ships and stayed hidden throughout the journey.

William Still, a free black member of the Philadelphia Vigilance Committee, described several escapes by boat in a book he wrote about the Underground Railroad. During one escape, a group of five slaves sailed from Portsmouth, Virginia, and reached Philadelphia. Still wrote that "every rod of rowing was attended with [great] peril." Another slave almost died sailing from Georgia to the North. He hid in a tiny area in the front of the ship that filled with salt water throughout the trip.

Between 1803 and 1866, about 14 percent of the sailors on ships sailing from such major ports as New York, Baltimore, Philadelphia, and Savannah were African American, both enslaved and free.

FAMOUS FUGITIVES AND THEIR ESCAPES

Some African Americans were light-skinned and could pretend to be white. If they had the courage, they could walk onto a ship or board a train as paying customers. Assuming they could play their role for several days, they stepped off the boat or train as free people.

In 1848, an abolitionist named Daniel Drayton tried to pull off the largest sea escape of enslaved African Americans—and perhaps the largest escape ever in the United States. For $100, he hired the sailing ship *Pearl* to take 77 slaves from Washington, D.C., to Philadelphia. The *Pearl* sailed at night under a light fog. After a short distance, the wind died down, leaving the ship sitting in the Potomac River. The next day, a steamship found the *Pearl* and took the slaves back to Washington. Some of the fugitives were sold to plantations further south, while Drayton and the ship's captain spent four and a half years in jail. Drayton later explained why he took part in the Underground Railroad: "The satisfaction that I have is this: What I did, and what I attempted to do, was my protest . . . against the infamous and atrocious doctrine that there can be any such thing as property in man!"

One of the most famous escapes featured a light-skinned African-American woman and her darker-skinned husband. Ellen and William Craft were slaves in Georgia who ran away from their masters. Ellen dressed as a white man and pretended to be injured and ill. William posed as her slave. In December 1848, they began their escape north.

Traveling by train, the Crafts met many whites. One offered to buy William. Ellen, playing her part, said, "I don't wish to sell, sir; I cannot get on well without him." From Charleston, the Crafts sailed to North Carolina and then traveled by train to Baltimore and Philadelphia. In Philadelphia, they met with workers on the Underground Railroad. The abolitionists told them to go to Boston, and from there, the Crafts went on to Canada.

Henry "Box" Brown is greeted in Philadelphia by Frederick Douglass and other abolitionists in this lithograph from 1850.

Some fugitives found a way to avoid seeing anyone on their trip north. Several slaves bought large wooden boxes and had themselves shipped to free states. The best known of these fugitives was Henry "Box" Brown. In 1848, he sealed himself inside a wooden box, along with some biscuits and water. From inside the box, Brown used a small tool called a gimlet to drill tiny air holes. A friend sent the box by train from Richmond, Virginia, to Philadelphia. There, members of the Vigilance Committee received a message that "your case of goods is shipped and will arrive tomorrow morning." They sheltered Brown before he headed farther north to Boston.

Like the Crafts and Henry "Box" Brown, Frederick Douglass also escaped by train. As a slave in Baltimore, Douglass helped build ships. In 1838 disguised as a sailor, he boarded a train heading to Philadelphia. He also borrowed legal papers from a free black sailor.

Douglass went from Philadelphia to New York, where he received aid from David Ruggles, a free African American and a member of the Underground Railroad. As Douglass wrote, Ruggles was "attending to a number of other fugitive slaves, devising ways and means for their successful escape." Ruggles helped Douglass reach New Bedford, Massachusetts. Eventually, Douglass became a leading abolitionist, and in 1846, some friends helped him buy his freedom.

The Need for Secrecy

Frederick Douglass first wrote about his escape in 1845, but he did not give details about his experience. He thought that people working on the Underground Railroad had turned it into an "upperground railroad" by talking about their activities so much. Douglass wrote,

I see and feel assured that those open declarations are a positive evil to the slaves remaining, who are seeking to escape. They do nothing towards enlightening the slave, whilst they do much towards enlightening the master. They stimulate him to greater watchfulness, and enhance his power to capture his slave. . . . We owe something to the slave south of the [Mason-Dixon] line as well as to those north of it; and in aiding the latter on their way to freedom, we should be careful to do nothing which would be likely to hinder the former from escaping from slavery.

After joining the abolitionist movement, Douglass worked on the Underground Railroad. His home in Rochester, New York, was an important stop on the railroad in that region for fugitives making their way to Canada. Western New York was home to many white abolitionists who supported the railroad, such as Gerrit Smith. The members hid runaways in local swamps or in cellars. At his home, Douglass took in slaves who could not find room at other stops in the region. He once hid 11 slaves in his house. He later wrote, "It was the largest group I ever had and it was difficult for me to give shelter, food, and money for so many . . . but it had to be done so they could be moved on immediately to Canada."

FIGHTING THE UNDERGROUND RAILROAD

Runaways troubled slave owners more than any other problem they faced. One master wrote in his diary, "I had rather a negro would do anything Else than runaway." Some masters tried to keep slaves from escaping by treating them well. However, even the best master's treatment was not worth a slave's loss of freedom.

Starting in the late 18th century, every Southern state passed laws regarding fugitive slaves. An 1839 law in Arkansas said that slaves could not go more than 20 miles (32 km) from their master's home without a pass. Slaves who went beyond that distance could be seized by any white citizen and brought to legal officials. The citizen received a $15 reward. Texas slave catchers earned $50 for each slave they returned to the state.

The slave states also passed laws creating special patrols. The patrollers had the legal right to search almost anywhere for fugitive slaves. In 1808, one patroller described searching slave cabins for weapons and noted that he had the power to "apprehend every negro whom we found from his home; & if he made any resistance, or ran from us, to fire on him immediately, unless he could be stopped by other means."

Slaves found a way to fight back against the Southern patrols. They sometimes strung ropes or grapevines across a road to trip up the patrollers' horses and send the riders crashing to the ground.

The patrols were often led by prominent citizens. Members included both slave owners and poor whites who did not own slaves. The patrollers carried guns, whips, and ropes as they walked or rode through Southern towns and cities. The patrols looked for slaves who were out after curfew, and they punished slaves who aided fugitives.

One of the most common tools used for capturing a runaway was a public advertisement. Masters bought ads in newspapers or posted signs in public places. The ads described how the slaves looked, acted, and dressed. They also listed possible places where the slaves might have gone—often, the town where relatives or a former master lived. The masters noted the slaves' skills that might help them avoid capture. One Louisiana master, for example, noted that his slave Robert was "very intelligent and active, speaks good

English a little French, but understands it very well." The ads for runaways included the reward offered for their return.

Slave catchers were another tool masters used to track down runaways. These slave catchers charged a fee for each day they worked and for each mile they traveled. They often used packs of bloodhounds. According to an English visitor in South Carolina, the dogs could be "ferocious . . . and savage-looking animals." Runaways tried to fool the hounds by wading through streams so the dogs would lose their scent.

One legal battle between abolitionists and slave owners reached the U.S. Supreme Court, the most powerful court in the country. In 1837, Edward Prigg, a slave catcher from Maryland, crossed into Pennsylvania to track down a fugitive slave. He did not have a warrant, a legal document needed to arrest someone, but he still took the slave back to Maryland. Prigg claimed that under the Fugitive Slave Act of 1793, he did not need a warrant. Members of the Underground Railroad in Pennsylvania disagreed, and they convinced state officials to arrest him for kidnapping. The Supreme Court eventually found that Prigg's actions were legal.

Most slave catchers worked in the South, since few masters had the money to pay for a long trip to the North. The slave catchers who did go north could turn violent as they sought their targets. One fugitive described how slave catchers entered the homes of African-American families and "would present pistols, and strike and knock down men and women." At least one free African American who worked for the Underground Railroad was killed for his service. Farther north, however, the workers on the railroad faced less danger—certainly less than the slaves they helped.

6

Life in the "Promised Land"

Fugitive slaves ride for freedom in this 1860 painting by artist Eastman Johnson. In the days long before television and other mass media, Johnson's paintings of black people in the South introduced many Americans to the plight of slaves.

THE PROMISED LAND

Many slaves saw their quest for freedom in religious terms. The slaves believed that God would help them reach their goal, the "Promised Land"—Africa, Canada, or the northern United States. Enslaved Christians wrote songs, called spirituals, that reflected their faith in God. The songs also offered a hope for freedom. The words in some songs could be understood as a sort of code that told slaves what to do in order to reach the North.

A group of slaves on a Southern plantation sings together. Slaves sang to celebrate their religious beliefs and to communicate their hopes for freedom in ways that their masters did not understand.

Frederick Douglass wrote about several songs that slaves sang as they prepared to run away. The lyrics of one talked about reaching "sweet Canaan." In the Bible, Canaan was the land to which, according to God's promise, Moses led the Israelites after they escaped from bondage in Egypt. In spirituals, Canaan sometimes meant heaven. But when Douglass sang about Canaan, he said, "We meant to reach the *north*—and the north was our Canaan."

Some songs served as a code for runaways already on the Underground Railroad. Harriet Tubman, one of the most famous conductors, escaped from her Maryland master in 1849 and then made several trips back into the South to help other fugitives. Tubman sang a special song to let hiding runaways know that she was coming and the path was clear. Another song, "Go Down Moses," told slaves to stay hidden.

LIFE IN THE NORTH

For many fugitives heading north, their destination was a black community, such as

Looking to the Sky

On their journeys north, runaway slaves knew to follow the North Star, which meant keeping the star in front of them as they traveled. As long as they headed north, they were going in the right direction. To locate the North Star in the sky, slaves could follow a line created by two of the stars in the Big Dipper. The slaves called the Big Dipper the "Drinking Gourd." As Africans had long done in their homelands, enslaved African Americans used hollow gourds to hold water. One song sung on the Underground Railroad told runaways "the old man is awaitin' for to carry you to freedom if you follow the drinking gourd."

those in Ohio and Indiana. African-American communities also appeared farther north. Ralph Smith, a white abolitionist and Secretary of the Philadelphia Vigilance Committee, bought land for free blacks in New Jersey. The new town, called Free Haven, welcomed enslaved people who managed to leave the South. A nearby town, Timbuctoo, was also home to both free African Americans and runaways.

Many escaped slaves who settled in the North had useful skills. They could find work with existing companies or start their own businesses. William Craft wrote that when he and his wife, Ellen, reached Boston, he was "employed as cabinet-maker and furniture broker, and my wife at her needle."

In 1840, almost all African Americans living in the North were free. In the South, just 8 percent were free. Mississippi had the smallest percentage of free blacks—just 0.7 percent. Delaware was the slave state with the largest population of free blacks, with 86.7 percent.

Although some runaways did find a decent life in the North, escaped slaves still had to worry about slave catchers and kidnappers. All blacks, both fugitive and free, faced racism. Many whites did not think blacks were equal to them and did not want to work with or live near African Americans.

As slavery ended in the North, some states, such as Illinois, tried to prevent free blacks from entering. Many Northern states would not let free blacks vote or send their children to public schools. Blacks were unwelcome in many white churches, and they were sometimes prevented from holding skilled jobs. Many white business owners would hire blacks only for such work as digging ditches or serving food in restaurants. Many free blacks also worked as servants.

In 1831, French writer Alexis de Tocqueville visited the United States and later noted that racism "appears to be stronger in the states that have abolished slavery than in those where it still exists." In 1850, Jacob Miller, a U.S. senator from New Jersey, called fugitives "worthless slaves" who remained in the state "to the annoyance of our people." Even many Northern abolitionists who supported the Underground Railroad had racist views. Theodore Parker of Massachusetts said that African Americans were not as smart as whites and had less of "that instinct for freedom which is so strong in [Northern Europeans]."

The prejudice of whites against blacks sometimes led to violence. In 1831, sailors visiting Providence, Rhode Island, got into a fight with free blacks. In the riot that followed, several people were killed. Ten years later, a riot erupted in Cincinnati after an argument between Irish immigrants and free African Americans turned violent. The violence lasted for several days. "Men were wounded on both sides and carried off," the paper wrote, "and many reported dead." The military had to be called in to restore order.

Slave owners in the South told their slaves about the violence and difficult living conditions they might face if they fled to free states. Slave owners also described the cold Northern winters. By convincing their slaves that life was even harder for blacks in the distant North, the masters discouraged the slaves from trying to escape. Frederick Douglass wrote that the real, geographical distance between the slave states and free states was less than "the imagined distance [that] was, to our ignorance, much greater."

LIFE IN CANADA

For some fleeing slaves, the North Star was not only a light in the sky that showed the way to freedom. The North Star was another name for Canada, where many fugitive slaves settled. Some went directly to Canada on the Underground Railroad. Others moved across the border after first living as free people in the northern United States.

Most blacks moving from the United States to Canada settled in the province of Ontario. Ontario was the closest province to several free states, including Michigan, Wisconsin, Ohio, Pennsylvania, and New York. Many Underground Railroad routes through those states led to cities along the Great Lakes, which separate Canada from the United States. At certain spots, slaves only had to cross narrow rivers to reach Canada. Many fugitives who reached Ontario settled near the border, close to Buffalo and Detroit. A few became pioneers and went deep into the Canadian forests. In some cases, once one black family settled in an area, others followed. William Jackson and his father were two African Americans who settled in the woods outside Canestogo, Ontario. Jackson said that "for many years scarcely any white people came in, but fugitive slaves came in, in great numbers, and cleared the land."

Escaped slaves who settled in one region sometimes worked together to build their own towns. One of the best-known of these towns was Dawn, Ontario. In 1838, several hundred free blacks decided they wanted to work for themselves, rather than for white business owners. A key feature of the new town was a school that taught African-American children skills so they could do more than farm. Money donated by abolitionists helped Dawn get started, and by the 1850s the town had about 500 residents. Their businesses included a sawmill and a rope factory.

Fugitive slaves and free blacks who went to Canada also lived among whites in cities and towns. Toronto, Ontario, was one destination, especially if a fugitive had a useful skill. Charles Peyton Lucas settled in Toronto in 1850. He was a blacksmith, described by one local resident as "at the head of his trade." Thornton Blackburn fled his master in Kentucky and settled in Toronto. In 1837, he opened the city's first successful taxi service.

Starting in 1826, Toronto's African-American community had its own churches. The first of them, a Baptist church, played a role in the Underground Railroad. Its founding members had escaped slavery, and they worked to help other enslaved people reach Canada and win their freedom.

The Baptist church in Toronto founded by former U.S. slaves was the first Baptist church in the city and, most likely, the first in Ontario. It still exists today and is known as the First Baptist Church.

Josiah Henson helped found Dawn. One of the fugitives helped by Levi Coffin, Henson fled his Maryland master and reached Canada in 1830. In 1849, he published his autobiography, describing his life as a slave, a fugitive, and a free man in Canada. Detailing his joy when he came to Canada, Henson wrote, "When my feet first touched the Canadian shore, I threw myself on the ground, rolled in the sand, seized handfuls of it and kissed them." By some reports, Henson served as the model for Uncle Tom, one of the major characters in Harriet Beecher Stowe's antislavery novel *Uncle Tom's Cabin.* In 1983, Henson's face appeared on a Canadian stamp. He was the first black person to receive that honor.

Josiah Henson was born into slavery in 1789 in Maryland. After being sold three times before he was 18, Henson saved $350 to buy his freedom. When his master raised the price to $1,000, Henson fled to Canada with his wife and four children.

LEGAL ISSUES

In 1833, Great Britain passed a law ending slavery throughout all its lands. These lands included Canada, which did not become a separate country until 1867. More U.S. slaves began to head to Canada, although they still faced the chance that they would be returned to the United States.

A famous incident in 1837 showed the legal risks of fleeing to Canada. A slave named Solomon Moseby escaped from Kentucky to Buffalo, then reached Niagara, Canada. Moseby's master tracked him down in Canada and demanded that he be extradited, or legally forced to return to the United States. The master accused Moseby of stealing a horse, as well as running away.

Since slavery was illegal under British law, running away was not a crime. Canadian officials would not extradite Moseby merely because he was a fugitive. Stealing a horse, however, was a crime, and so Canadian officials arrested him and investigated the case. Moseby's defenders said that there was no proof he had stolen the horse and that his master would not have taken the time and money to pursue a mere horse thief. His real interest was getting Moseby, who was a free man now under British law. If Moseby were extradited, one legal document argued, "no runaway slave will either now or henceforth be safe in a British colony."

Despite this argument, the Canadian officials concluded that Moseby should be extradited for stealing the horse. A group of free African Americans living in Niagara protested. During a riot outside his jail, Moseby was able to escape. He eventually reached England. The next year, Great Britain tightened its extradition law. From then on, someone who alleged that a runaway had committed a crime had to show proof. Only fugitives who did something that was illegal in Canada would face extradition to the United States.

With the end of slavery throughout the British empire, some former slaves moved to England. Others, such as Frederick Douglass and William Wells Brown, traveled there.

Brown spoke to English audiences about the evils of slavery. In 1849, he told one crowd that he "would rather be a beggar in England than the best conditioned slave in America." British abolitionists led the effort to end the international slave trade and spoke out against slavery in the United States.

THOUGHTS OF AFRICA

During the 19th century, both whites and free blacks discussed the idea of colonization. Under this plan, African Americans would travel to Africa and set up their own colonies. A group of free blacks from Canada did this in 1792, sailing for Sierra Leone. Over the next three decades, free blacks and fugitives, mostly from British lands, settled Sierra Leone.

In 1816, Southern and Northern whites founded the American Colonization Society, intending to locate land in Africa where free blacks could settle. In 1821, the society helped a group of free African Americans buy land in West Africa. This colony eventually became the nation of Liberia. During the next decade, about 2,600 African Americans settled there. Other settlers were slaves who managed to escape from slave ships. Some former fugitives who had settled in the North or in Canada also decided to move on to Africa.

Founding members of the American Colonization Society included Francis Scott Key, who wrote "The Star Spangled Banner"; Andrew Jackson, a future U.S. president; and Daniel Webster, a well-known U.S. politician and public speaker from Massachusetts.

Monrovia, the capital of Liberia in Africa, is shown as it appeared about 1832. Liberia was established by former slaves with the financial backing of white Americans.

Colonization appealed to some U.S. slave owners. If free blacks moved to Africa, they could not fight for the abolition of slavery or help slaves escape. Some whites who opposed slavery yet still had racist beliefs also supported colonization. They did not necessarily want free blacks or fugitives living among them or enjoying all the rights that whites had. Other abolitionists did not think that African Americans would fit into a society dominated by whites. Some free African Americans agreed. They believed that former slaves and free-born blacks would be happier living apart from whites.

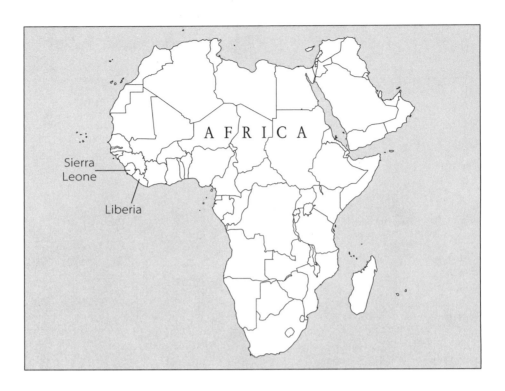

The countries of Sierra Leone and Liberia were created so that former slaves could return to Africa. The British established the first slave refugee colony in Sierra Leone in 1787. Liberia became an independent country in 1816.

Many abolitionists, however, opposed colonization. They argued that free blacks deserved the same rights as whites and should not be forced to move to a foreign country just because their ancestors had once lived there. Black abolitionists in particular disliked the idea that somehow free blacks were not truly American and did not deserve the same rights as white citizens. In 1817, a group of free blacks in Virginia declared, "We prefer being colonized in the most remote corner of the land of our nativity, to being exiled to a foreign country."

7

The Railroad Reaches Its Peak

A group of runaway slaves and Underground Railroad conductors
hide in the woods while slave hunters search nearby. White abolitionists
and free blacks often worked together to hide fugitives
and help them avoid capture

THE COMPROMISE OF 1850

The success of the Underground Railroad during the 1840s upset many Southerners. Even though only a small percentage of slaves ran away and reached the North, the slave owners detested anyone who helped slaves escape. They focused their anger on white Northern abolitionists, even though not all of them were active in the railroad.

The issue of fugitive slaves entered national politics in 1850. California, New Mexico, and Utah wanted to enter the Union. The United States had acquired these areas with its victory in the U.S.-Mexican War (1846–1848). Since Mexico had already outlawed slavery, these lands were free territories. Southern lawmakers opposed admitting California to the Union as a free state. Also at stake was whether slavery would be allowed in other western lands.

As U.S. lawmakers debated the issue, some people suggested that the country should split and form two nations. One would allow slavery and the other would be free. A few abolitionists thought the North would be better off pursuing this idea of disunion. One of them, Wendell Phillips, expressed this view when he wrote, "No union with slaveholders!"

The Compromise of 1850 outlawed the slave trade in Washington, D.C., though slavery itself remained legal there.

Most lawmakers, however, wanted to preserve the Union. Led by Senator Henry Clay of Kentucky, Congress passed a series of laws called the Compromise of 1850. As part of the compromise, California entered the Union as a free state. New Mexico and Utah were made territories, and their citizens could decide for themselves whether or not to allow slavery. To satisfy Southern slave owners, Congress passed a new law regarding the return of fugitive slaves. Many lawmakers hoped the compromise would end arguments over slavery, but the debate—and anger—were far from over.

THE FUGITIVE SLAVE ACT OF 1850

The new Fugitive Slave Act replaced the old one of 1793. Under the new law, anyone who helped fugitives escape faced heavy fines and jail sentences. New federal workers called commissioners were put in charge of returning slaves to their masters. The commissioners could ignore state or local laws that helped runaways. African Americans accused of being runaways had almost no legal rights, and free blacks caught under the law could not offer evidence to prove that they were not slaves. To Northerners who opposed slavery, the most unpopular part of the law was Section 5. It said that "all good citizens are hereby commanded to aid and assist in the prompt and efficient execution of this law whenever their services may be required." Citizens who refused to help masters or slave catchers capture fugitives could be arrested.

Congress approved the new Fugitive Slave Act in September 1850. Across the North, black and white abolitionists united in opposing the new law. In some cases, free blacks prepared to defend themselves and fugitives who reached the North. A Rochester, New York, newspaper reported that free blacks "were pricing and buying fire arms

. . . with the avowed intention of using them against the ministers of the law."

The Fugitive Slave Act of 1850 had an immediate effect on fugitives living in the North. Many fled to Canada or Great Britain. By the end of the year, Canadian abolitionists reported that almost 5,000 African Americans had reached their country since the law was passed. Some slaves also fled to Mexico. As in Canada, some of these runaways founded their own communities. Other fugitives in Mexico married local residents and settled in existing towns.

FIGHTING THE LAW

Boston in 1850 was a center of Northern abolitionism. It was also the home of several hundred fugitive slaves, including such well-known runaways as Ellen and William Craft. The Crafts had publicly opposed the new Fugitive Slave Act, and their former master sent two men to catch them. Boston's abolitionists vowed to protect the Crafts. President Millard Fillmore ordered U.S. troops to go to Boston to arrest the

Crafts. Before the troops arrived, the Boston Vigilance Committee helped the Crafts reach Canada and then England.

Another Boston fugitive who escaped the slave catchers was Shadrach Minkins. He was working as a waiter when federal agents arrested him. When the news of his arrest spread, several hundred abolitionists came to his defense. A group of free African Americans stormed the courtroom where Minkins was held. They took him away and hid him with a black family in the city. A few days later, Minkins's rescuers took him to Canada. Eight people, both blacks and whites, were arrested for helping Minkins escape. The local jury found them innocent.

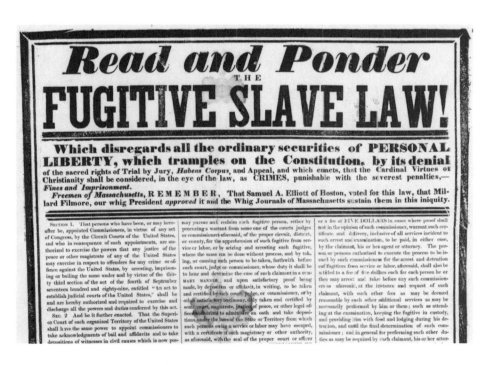

This poster from Massachusetts in 1850 condemns the Fugitive Slave Act and the Massachusetts politicians who voted for it.

During the 1850s, Northerners who opposed the Fugitive Slave Act made at least 80 known rescues or attempted rescues of captured fugitive slaves.

The battle between slave catchers and the people who helped fugitives sometimes turned violent. Pennsylvania was the site of several clashes. Since the state bordered several slave states, masters were more willing to send slave catchers there than to other parts of the North. Free blacks in Pennsylvania, as in other states, vowed to protect themselves and fugitives.

The first known violence against slave catchers after passage of the new Fugitive Slave Act occurred in the small Pennsylvania town of Christiana. In September 1851, a Maryland master named Edward Gorsuch was tracking down two slaves who had fled to Christiana. Gorsuch, arriving in town with several relatives, was greeted by about 100 free blacks armed with guns and farm tools. William Parker, who led the defenders, later wrote about what happened next. At one point, a U.S. marshal threatened to burn down Parker's home. "Burn us up and welcome," Parker said. "You can burn us, but you can't take us; before I give up, you will see my ashes scattered on the earth." A gunfight soon erupted. Gorsuch was killed, and several other people were wounded. The battle was later called the Christiana Riot.

About a month after the violence in Christiana, a large mob came to the defense of William McHenry. Also known as Jerry, he had fled his master in Missouri and reached Syracuse, New York. As many as 5,000 people protested his arrest. A small group of abolitionists, both black and white, broke into the police building where McHenry was held. One of the guards, fearing for his life, jumped from a second-story window and broke his arm. McHenry's rescuers managed to get him to Canada.

The defenders of fugitives were not always successful. In 1854, free blacks and whites united to try to rescue Anthony Burns, a slave who had reached Boston. The rescuers killed a U.S. law officer but failed to get Burns away. He was taken to court, where government officials called in more than 1,500 troops to keep order during his trial. Burns was returned to his master in Virginia and placed on sale. Fortunately, he was bought by abolitionists, who freed him.

DARING RESCUES

The Fugitive Slave Act influenced the thinking of one of the most famous conductors on the Underground Railroad: Harriet Tubman. She had just fled from Maryland to Pennsylvania when the law was passed. Like many free African Americans and white abolitionists, Tubman questioned the U.S. government. The law seemed to show that U.S. leaders would cooperate with slave owners rather than try to end slavery. Tubman said, "I wouldn't trust Uncle Sam [the government] with my people no longer." Like many members of the railroad, she realized that Canada was the only safe place for fugitives.

Throughout the 1850s, Tubman made a series of trips into the South to help enslaved people reach the North and then move on to Canada. Her first trip was in 1850, when she traveled to Baltimore to help her niece and her two children escape to freedom. Tubman's next few trips were also to aid her own relatives, but in December 1851, she helped 11 strangers escape from slavery—a dangerous feat. Also helping in the rescue were some of the best-known stationmasters on the Underground Railroad, including William Still of Pennsylvania and Thomas Garrett of Delaware.

American abolitionist Harriet Tubman was photographed in 1895 at the age of 72. Tubman died in 1913.

Tubman developed a routine for her work. She and her "passengers" traveled on back roads and only at night. She preferred to work during the winter months, when the nights were longer and local residents were more likely to stay inside. At times, Tubman rode the real railroad for Underground Railroad work. She took trains into the South, hoping people would assume that she was a free black, rather than a fugitive coming to help other slaves escape. To pay for her efforts, Tubman worked in the North as a cook or maid. She also received some help from Northern abolitionists.

Tubman demonstrated her bravery and toughness through

her many trips south. She knew she faced arrest, yet often had to sneak past law officials. One time, Tubman and some fugitives hid in a wagon to pass by police patrols. On another trip, she and about 25 fugitives hid all day in a swamp. One

fugitive wanted to return home. Tubman reminded him that all the runaways had pledged to stick together until they reached the North. At night, the man refused to leave the swamp. Tubman aimed a gun at the man's head and said, "You go on or you die." The reluctant runaway decided to go on. Thanks to Tubman's leadership, he eventually reached Canada.

EFFECTS OF THE FUGITIVE SLAVE ACT

The Fugitive Slave Act seemed to have some effect in reducing the number of runaways. Historians have suggested that the Fugitive Slave Act had its greatest impact as propaganda—information or actions meant to shape what people think or do. Neither the government nor the slave owners really expected to capture many fugitives. The slave owners simply wanted the government to acknowledge that slavery was constitutional. Northern politicians, meanwhile, backed the new law in exchange for Southern support on their favorite issues.

Southern lawmakers who supported the Fugitive Slave Act also saw its value as propaganda. If the Northern states did not accept the law and help catch fugitives, the South could accuse the Northerners of being disloyal and ignoring the Constitution. Southern leaders would have an issue they could use to unite the South against the abolitionist movement. The reaction to the Fugitive Slave Act in both regions of the country increased the tensions that led to the Civil War.

The single greatest piece of propaganda that emerged after the Fugitive Slave Act was *Uncle Tom's Cabin*. This book by Harriet Beecher Stowe gave many Northern readers their first look at slavery. It described the violence slaves faced from cruel masters. The book also specifically addressed the Fugitive Slave Act and runaway slaves. One character, a U.S. senator from Ohio, votes for the law, but then helps a fugitive escape and win her freedom.

The impact of Stowe's book was not limited to the United States. In the early 1850s, Great Britain was considering returning some U.S. slaves who reached Canada. After reading *Uncle Tom's Cabin,* members of the British royal family decided that the British government should continue to protect runaways in Canada.

Uncle Tom's Cabin became a best seller in the United States and Europe, selling 300,000 copies in one year. The book increased antislavery feelings in the North and further fueled Southern anger with the abolitionist movement. During the Civil War, President Abraham Lincoln supposedly called Stowe "the little lady who started this big war."

8

The Last Fugitives

Like many escaped slaves, this group is traveling north at night to avoid
capture. During the 1850s, new laws were passed to make it more
difficult for slaves to remain free even if they reached Northern states.

THE KANSAS-NEBRASKA ACT

In 1854, Congress passed the Kansas-Nebraska Act. The law let settlers in the territories of Kansas and Nebraska decide whether or not they would allow slavery. Kansas bordered the slave state of Missouri, and runaways from that state sometimes fled westward into Kansas. Missourians hoped that settlers from their state could dominate the politics in Kansas and vote to make slavery legal there. Across the South, slave owners welcomed any law that might increase the number of slave states. More slave states meant more lawmakers in Congress to defend slavery.

The Kansas-Nebraska Act overturned part of the Missouri Compromise of 1820. Under that law, slavery was not allowed above the latitude of 36° 30'—an imaginary line that ran along the southern border of Missouri. Both Kansas and Nebraska were north of that line.

Abolitionists from New England and other Northern states encouraged antislavery settlers to move to Kansas, where some people who opposed slavery already lived. Still, these settlers were outnumbered by Missourians and other Southerners who supported slavery. During elections, some Missourians crossed into Kansas and illegally voted for proslavery lawmakers. These representatives soon voted to execute anyone caught helping fugitive slaves. Antislavery Kansans elected their own governor and lawmakers, and in 1855, the supporters of the two sides sometimes battled. Fighting continued for several years, and the territory was nicknamed "Bleeding Kansas."

This map of Kansas and Nebraska shows how the territories looked in 1854. It also shows the Missouri Compromise line of 1820. Slavery was not allowed north of the line. The dates on the map represent either the year a state was admitted to the Union or the year a region was organized into a U.S. territory.

One white, Northern abolitionist who went to Kansas was John Brown. He wanted Kansas to be free, so it could become a final stop for fugitives on the Underground Railroad. Brown was willing to do anything to achieve his goals. That included killing five Kansas settlers who lived in a town that supported slavery. (The five men did not own slaves themselves.) Brown also hoped to build Underground Railroad stations that would serve as armed forts and convince Southern slave owners not to settle along the frontier.

THE DRED SCOTT CASE

Not all slaves went North as runaways. Slaves sometimes traveled with their masters into free states. During the 1830s, some Northern courts had ruled that slaves who spent time in free states could legally claim their freedom. Some slave owners did not know about these legal rulings. Others ignored them, assuming their slaves would not try to use the law to win their freedom.

In 1857, the U.S. Supreme Court debated the issue of slaves entering free states and territories. In the Dred Scott case, the Court ruled that slaves could not become free by traveling with their masters to a free state or territory. The Court said that slaves were property and did not have legal rights. Even free blacks, the Court said, were "not intended to be included in the constitution for the enjoyment of any personal rights or benefits."

A Long Legal Battle

A slave most likely born in Virginia, Dred Scott eventually ended up in Missouri. From there, his master took him and Scott's future wife into Illinois and the free territory of Wisconsin in the 1830s. The master eventually took both slaves back to Missouri. In 1846, Scott argued that under Missouri law, he and his wife should be freed, since they had spent time in a free state and territory. One Missouri court disagreed; another said the couple should be freed. In the U.S. Supreme Court, the final opinion of the court was written by Chief Justice Roger Taney. A former slave owner, Taney supported the legal rights of slave owners and shared many of the racist views on African Americans common at the time.

The Dred Scott decision meant that slaves could not expect legal protection if they ran away in a free state or territory. For abolitionists, the decision strengthened their desire to confront slave catchers. Free blacks saw the ruling as an attack on them. Charles Lenox Remond of Boston said African Americans "owe no allegiance to a country which grinds us under its iron hoof and treats us like dogs."

ACTIVE YEARS

As violence and political conflict went on around them, members of the Underground Railroad continued their work. In Northern cities, African-American vigilance committees and white abolitionists continued to guide fugitives to Canada. Rescue missions continued in the North as well.

By one estimate, from 15,000 to 20,000 African Americans, both fugitive and free, settled in Canada between 1850 and 1860.

New stations on the railroad opened. Some people joined the effort to help fugitives as a response to the Fugitive Slave Act, Bleeding Kansas, and the Dred Scott decision. These Americans wanted to show their anger over slavery and assert that sometimes a person must break the law in order to do what is truly right and just. In 1855, William Tallman, a wealthy, white lawyer, began building a beautiful new home

In Philadelphia, an African-American woman found a new way to help fugitives. In 1858, Henrietta Bowers Duterte became the first black woman to serve as an undertaker in that city. She hid runaways inside caskets to help them avoid slave catchers.

in Janesville, Wisconsin. When the large brick house was finished two years later, it featured secret hiding places for fugitives in the attic and the basement.

To show their disregard for the Fugitive Slave Act, some workers on the Underground Railroad openly wrote about their activities in newspapers. In Syracuse, New York, abolitionists published an article telling readers that J. W. Loguen, a former slave, ran the local Underground Railroad station. Throughout the 1850s, Loguen gave detailed public accounts of his efforts. His station was sometimes called the most open in the country, and as many as 1,500 slaves passed through it.

THE COMING OF THE CIVIL WAR

As the 1850s progressed, Americans feared that slavery would rip apart the United States. Southern lawmakers and slaveholders wanted to protect slavery at all costs. A growing number of Northerners wanted to halt its spread to new states and territories and perhaps end it everywhere in the country. The arguments over slavery led to the formation of a new political party, the Republicans. Its members included abolitionists and workers on the Underground Railroad.

In 1860, the Republicans chose Abraham Lincoln as their candidate for president of the United States. Lincoln wanted to limit the spread of slavery. However, he also promised Southerners that he would not threaten their legal right to own slaves. Slaveholders did not trust Lincoln to keep his promise. They also believed that he would not or could not limit the work of abolitionists and members of the Underground Railroad. In November, Lincoln won a four-way race for president, and before the end of the year, lawmakers in South Carolina reacted.

On December 20, 1860, South Carolina voted to secede, or break away, from the United States and form its own independent nation. In explaining this decision, the state's lawmakers focused on the issues of runaway slaves and constitutional law. The Constitution clearly said that states had to return fugitives to their masters. Northern states, however, consistently ignored laws that required them to capture and return enslaved people who ran away. Since the Northern states refused to return slaves

This Civil War poster from 1864 is aimed at encouraging blacks to join the Union cause and fight for the North.

to their owners, South Carolina lawmakers said that the Union created by the Constitution "has been deliberately broken and disregarded . . . and the consequence follows that South Carolina is released from her obligation" to remain in the Union. South Carolina also complained about the abolitionists and vigilance committees "whose avowed object is to disturb the peace and [hide] the property of the citizens of other states."

When the Civil War began, the Confederate South had 3.4 million slaves in a total population of 9.1 million people.

By February 1861, six states from the Deep South had joined South Carolina in seceding from the Union. A total of 11 slave states seceded and formed their own nation, the Confederate States of America (also called the Confederacy). Four slave states chose not to secede: Maryland, Delaware, Missouri, and Kentucky. They were known as the border states, since they sat along the border between the United States and the Confederacy.

President Lincoln said that the Confederate states had no right under the Constitution to secede. He was determined to assert that he was president of all the states, not just the North. He therefore refused to withdraw U.S. troops from Fort Sumter, in Charleston, South Carolina. In April, Confederate forces attacked the fort. This attack was the beginning of the Civil War. The war was not intended to free slaves, but slavery was its root cause.

This 1862 illustration, called "Contraband of War," shows Union soldiers directing slaves who had come to them after the slaves had run away to the North during the Civil War.

FUGITIVES DURING WARTIME

Some slaves saw the confusion created by the war as a chance to run away. Masters tried to keep their slaves at home by telling them horror stories about Northerners. One slave recalled white Southerners telling slaves that Northerners "would harness [slaves] to carts and make them pull the carts around, in place of horses." Still, many slaves sought out Northern troops.

The slaves who ran away received a mixed reception when they reached Union forces. At times, the Northern soldiers returned them to their masters. Other officers allowed the slaves to stay with the army. In August 1861, the U.S. Congress made it the official Northern policy to keep any slaves the soldiers encountered because they were the property of rebels fighting the United States. These slaves and runaways who reached Union troops were known as contraband. At military camps, contraband slaves were soon digging ditches, preparing meals, and washing clothes.

Austin Bearse, a Massachusetts abolitionist, wrote about one unnamed fugitive who had fled to Canada. After the Emancipation Proclamation, he "returned to Boston, joined a colored regiment, went South, and was killed in battle. This slave proved a true patriot by sacrificing his life for his country."

In July 1862, Congress allowed free blacks to join the Union army. Then on January 1, 1863, President Lincoln issued the Emancipation Proclamation. Any slaves in states still under Confederate control were now free. Lincoln's order did not affect slaves in the border states or parts of the Confederacy already under Union control. Even more enslaved people in the South ran from their masters and joined up with Union troops. As many as 750,000 slaves fled their masters after Lincoln issued the Emancipation Proclamation. One happy slave said that a Union army camp "is now our Canada!"

THE END OF SLAVERY—AND THE UNDERGROUND RAILROAD

By the end of 1864, the war was almost over. Congress began to discuss ending slavery everywhere by amending, or changing, the U.S. Constitution. In December 1865, the Thirteenth Amendment was approved and added to the Constitution. The amendment outlawed slavery in any territory under U.S. control. In April 1865, the Confederate army surrendered. The Union victory meant that fugitives would no longer have to ride the Underground Railroad to find their freedom.

With slavery finally ended, former fugitive slaves such as Frederick Douglass and Harriet Tubman called for equal rights for all African Americans. White abolitionists such as Levi Coffin and Wendell Philips called for passage of the Fifteenth Amendment, which gave free black males the right to vote. (Women of all races would not receive a constitutional right to vote until 1920.)

Some members of the railroad began to write about the work they had done to help slaves escape in the years before the Civil War. In 1872, William Still wrote one of the first books on the Underground Railroad. The book was so popular that Still later published two more editions.

In 1898, Wilbur H. Siebert published the first major historical study of the Underground Railroad. Siebert's work inspired other historians to study the people and places that made up the Underground Railroad. Today, the world has a better understanding of the slaves who risked their lives to find freedom, and the people who helped them reach their goal.

Time Line

1502	The first known fugitive slave in the Americas jumps off a Spanish ship.
ca. 1605	The first maroon community, Palmares, is founded in Brazil.
1642	Virginia makes it illegal to help runaway servants.
1691	A Virginia law gives citizens the right to kill fugitives who resist arrest.
1693	Spain promises to grant freedom to any English slaves who reach Florida.
1775	The British royal governor in Virginia offers freedom to slaves who run away from their masters and fight for the British during the American Revolution.
1787	The U.S. Constitution requires that fugitive slaves must be returned to their masters. The Northwest Ordinance outlaws slavery in the Northwest Territory but also requires that fugitive slaves must be returned to their masters.
1792	Former U.S. slaves living in Canada found a colony in Sierra Leone, Africa.

1793	Congress passes the Fugitive Slave Act, which allows masters to track down fugitive slaves and fines anyone who helps runaways. Upper Canada passes a law that virtually ends slavery there.
1812–1815	During the War of 1812, Great Britain once again offers freedom to slaves who run away from their U.S. masters.
1829	Mexico ends slavery.
1831	Nat Turner leads a slave revolt in Virginia; afterward, slave states pass new laws restricting the actions of slaves. By one account, the system that helps runaways is given the name Underground Railroad.
1833	Great Britain abolishes slavery in all its lands, including Canada.
1835	The Philadelphia Vigilance Committee forms to aid free blacks and fugitive slaves.
1838	Former U.S. slaves who reached Canada found the town of Dawn. Frederick Douglass uses the Underground Railroad to reach Massachusetts.
1842	The U.S. Supreme Court rules that Northern states cannot pass laws that limit the Fugitive Slave Act of 1793.
1844	Jonathan Walker is arrested in Florida and branded for "stealing" slaves from their masters.

1850	Fugitive slave Harriet Tubman makes the first of many trips into the South to guide other slaves to freedom. The Compromise of 1850 admits California to the Union as a free state but allows slavery in the new western territories. Congress passes a new Fugitive Slave Act, which requires Northerners to help track down fugitives.
1851	In Christiana, Pennsylvania, members of the Underground Railroad kill a master hunting for two escaped slaves.
1857	In the *Dred Scott* case, the U.S. Supreme Court rules that all African Americans, whether slave or free, have no legal rights.
1860	Abraham Lincoln is elected president. South Carolina is the first of 11 slave states to secede from the Union.
1861	The Civil War begins in April. In August, Congress rules that U.S. troops will not return any fugitive slaves they encounter.
1863	President Lincoln frees the slaves in states still under Confederate control with the Emancipation Proclamation.
1864	Several Southern states abolish slavery.
1865	The Thirteenth Amendment, ending slavery across the United States, is added to the Constitution.

Glossary

abolitionist   A person who seeks an immediate end to slavery.

contraband   Fugitive slaves who came under the control of Union troops during the Civil War.

Deep South   Usually refers to the part of the United States that includes Alabama, Arkansas, Florida, Georgia, Louisiana, Mississippi, Texas, and parts of the Carolinas and Tennessee.

emancipation   The act of freeing slaves.

extradite   To legally force someone who has been accused of committing a crime to go from one jurisdiction or country to another.

Fifteenth Amendment   An amendment to the U.S. Constitution guaranteeing voting rights for all male citizens.

fugitive   A person who escapes from slave owners or law officials.

indenture   A contract that requires a person to work for a master for a certain number of years.

lynch   To murder by mob action, without a legal trial.

manumit   To free from slavery.

maroons   Fugitive slaves who started their own communities in remote areas.

plantation   A large farm that relied on slaves to produce one main crop.

prejudice   An unreasonable bias against or intolerance of others.

propaganda   Information or actions meant to shape what people think or do.

racism   Prejudice based on race.

spiritual   A folk hymn of a type developed by blacks in the American South that combined African and European elements and expressed deep emotion.

Thirteenth Amendment   An amendment to the U.S. Constitution prohibiting slavery.

warrant   A legal document that allows a law officer to arrest someone.

West Indies   A group of islands in the Caribbean Sea.

Further Reading

BOOKS

Currie, Stephen. *Escape from Slavery.* San Diego: Lucent Books, 2003.

Hansen, Joyce. *Freedom Roads: Searching for the Underground Railroad.* Chicago: Cricket Press, 2003.

Haskins, James, and Kathleen Benson. *Following Freedom's Star: The Story of the Underground Railroad.* New York: Benchmark, 2001.

Sullivan, George. *Harriet Tubman.* New York: Scholastic Reference, 2002.

Wolny, Philip. *The Underground Railroad: A Primary Source History of the Journey to Freedom.* New York: Rosen, 2004.

WEB SITES

National Underground Railroad Freedom Center. URL: http://www.freedomcenter.org/. Downloaded on May 23, 2005.

Our Shared History. "African-American Heritage: Underground Railroad." URL: http://www.cr.nps.gov/aahistory/ugrr/ugrr.htm. Downloaded on May 23, 2005.

Parks Canada. "The Underground Railroad in Canada." URL: http://www.pc.gc.ca/canada/proj/cfc-ugrr/index_e.asp. Downloaded on May 23, 2005.

PBS Online. "Africans in America." URL: http://www.pbs.org/wgbh/aia/home.html. Downloaded on May 23, 2005.

Index